MORE PRAISE FOR ... bounce

"Bounce is going to reorient the way you think about tackling business issues, keeping your team engaged, and winning in the marketplace." —DAVE BARGER,
President and CEO, JetBlue Airways Corporation

"Keith McFarland has written a brilliant and insightful work on how leaders should face adversity. It's a must-read for leaders in every field in these times which present daunting challenges and require strong people at the top."
—GENERAL ANTHONY C. ZINNI USMC (retired),
Former commander in chief, CENTCOM

"When the rules seem to be changing . . . Bounce can be just the provocation we need to rediscover our path to success."
—STEPHEN C. LUNDIN, PH.D.,
Author of the national bestseller *Fish!*

"A must-read that is truly inspiring . . . What's even more impressive than the storytelling are the takeaways that you'll instantly incorporate into your life. Consider this book's cover price small payment for the golden nuggets of wisdom you'll be carting off."
—JOSH BERMAN,
Cofounder, MySpace.com, and president, Slingshot Labs

. . . plus praise for Keith McFarland's first book, The Breakthrough Company

"Has the makings of a classic . . . McFarland successfully tackles the ever-present question for ambitious entrepreneurs: Just how do you go from small to big—and prosper?" —STEVE FORBES,
President and CEO, editor-in-chief, *Forbes*

bounce

THE
ART OF
TURNING
TOUGH TIMES
INTO TRIUMPH

Keith McFarland

Library of Congress Cataloging-in-Publication Data
is available upon request.

ISBN 978-0-692-18898-9

Printed in the United States of America

Design by Haylie Christensen

10 9 8 7 6 5 4 3 2 1

Second Edition

For the troops

contents

preface

nelson Mandela once told an interviewer that if
it weren't for the time he spent in prison, he
might never have developed the strength later necessary
to lead his nation out of apartheid. He was pointing to a
frequently overlooked but universal truth: It's often during
life's most difficult times that we discover our most critical
hidden strengths and that we forge our most important
capabilities.

Fortunately, you don't have to spend twenty-seven years
in prison to experience the formative power of adversity.
Life is full of challenges large and small—each an invitation
to retire old ways of thinking and to stretch toward new
and better solutions. Successful people harness the power of
adversity much like sailors harness the force of a threatening
wind, trimming their sails and leaning in hard.

The same is true for organizations. I spent the past
seven years studying the performance of more than seven
thousand leading growth companies. The top performers
had one interesting thing in common: Each went through

a period of pronounced difficulty—often serious enough to threaten the firm's very existence.

Great companies, I discovered, arise not from the absence of difficulty but rather from its vortex. How a company responds to these defining moments may be a better predictor of organizational strength and resilience than markets penetrated or competitors bested. As their organizations enter tough times, the best leaders are careful not to focus solely on survival. Instead, they guide their firms to ask the fundamental questions, to face facts that might have gone overlooked in more prosperous times, and to identify and integrate the new knowledge and insights that adversity can bring.

The story that follows is set in a business, but it might just as well have been set in a family, a church, an army platoon, or in the White House. For people in all kinds of institutions, the key question today is how do we turn tough times into triumph? And how do we help those around us do the same—how do we help them find their bounce?

the story

pothole on the road to greatness

i f ever Mike Maloney needed a workout, it was
now. His plane landed back at Logan Airport at
midnight, two hours late. He had left home at 6:00 A.M.
that morning in a blizzard to catch the 8:00 A.M. flight from
Boston to Omaha. Landing in the middle of the Midwest's
worst ice storm of the year, he drove an hour and a half
to Altech Corporation—an important customer that had
threatened to cancel its contract with his company just days
earlier.

Over the past year, profits at his company had
evaporated, and he was under pressure from the parent
company to turn things around. A recent spate of customer
defections was making things even worse.

Now, stopping by the office outside Boston on his way
home that night, Mike found a letter of resignation on his
desk from his vice president of operations. The last straw,
he thought. He was dead tired—but he knew Mary and the
girls would be fast asleep, and he was too keyed up to go
home. He drove a few blocks and swung his Lexus into the

snowy parking lot of the 24 Hour Fitness and parked in the yellow glow of a street lamp. He grabbed his gear bag off the backseat and headed inside. The gym looked deserted except for the girl at the front desk sleepily playing solitaire on the computer.

"Haven't seen much of you lately," someone shouted as he entered the locker room. Mike turned to see Joe Nicks sitting on a bench, untying his shoe, sweat running from his crew cut. Joe was a bulldog of a man, all neck and chest, his military head cropped flat as a tree stump. He and Mike had sometimes worked out together since Joe returned from his deployment in Afghanistan six months ago.

"I have been on the road every week for the past six weeks," Mike said wearily, adding with a smirk, "still living the dream."

"You keep that up, and you'll end up all weak, white, and pasty," chuckled Joe.

"We are just getting thrashed in the market right now, and I am spending all my time on planes trying to hold on to the customers we have and close some new deals," explained Mike. "Revenues were down fifteen percent last year, and the parent company is all over me like a cheap suit. Last year we cut all the fat, and now they want me to cut muscle and bone." Suddenly embarrassed that he was talking about his work problems, Mike changed the subject: "You just finishing up?"

"I just hit the weights for a bit," said Joe, "but I'll kick your butt on some cardio if you want."

They set up next to each other on the treadmills, and Mike punched in his weight and selected a tough interval workout. He felt a rush of adrenaline as Joe's treadmill whirred to life—and hoped that his determination to outlast Joe would take his mind off work.

They worked out silently side by side for about a half hour. All this travel had made it tough for Mike to get in a regular workout, and he found himself struggling to keep up the pace with Joe. Sweat soaked his shirt and stung his eyes.

"Sounds like things are pretty tough in the trenches right now," said Joe.

Mike was panting so hard he wasn't sure he would be able to carry on a conversation, but his pride pushed him to respond, and before he knew it, he was telling Joe the whole story. A year ago he had left a job in which, for eight years, he had been running a medium-size specialty technology manufacturer, to join the CRX Group. But shortly after he took over his division of CRX, the bottom fell out of the market, and Mike and his team went into survival mode. Rachel, the parent company CEO, was pushing him to make deep staffing cuts, and Mike worried that if he did so his division might lose a crucial position in the market that it might never regain. And over the past few weeks, it seemed that his company was really beginning to unravel. With all his traveling, he was losing touch with what was going on in the office. People seemed listless, distracted, and discouraged. And now his VP of operations, one of his veteran team members, had submitted his resignation. People at the company were already on the edge; this would certainly send them over it.

"It could be that your business just turned onto the road to greatness," said Joe.

"Right," smirked Mike, but when he looked over at Joe, he realized he was serious. "Well, if this is greatness, I could go for a little mediocrity," Mike added. Joe just smiled and nodded and didn't say anything for a few minutes.

Mike was gasping for air when the treadmill timer hit fifty-five minutes and he pushed the cooldown button and was relieved when Joe did the same. "If our company is on the road to greatness, we've definitely hit a pothole." Mike said, panting heavily.

"Or you're ready to bounce," said Joe. His treadmill flashed sixty minutes and whirred to a stop.

"Bounce?" Mike asked, wiping his face with a towel. "What do you mean?"

"Bounce is always the first step in real progress, " responded Joe, "Answer two questions, and you'll see what I'm talking about," Joe said.

"OK," said Mike.

anatomy of a bounce

oe leaned over and looked him in the eye.

"**Question number one:** What is the one quality you most like about yourself?"

Mike thought for a moment, a little embarrassed about being asked to talk about his own qualities.

"Gee, I don't know, I guess it's that I'm adaptable—I just adapt to whatever life throws at me," replied Mike.

"Great. **Question number two:** Can you think of a time in your life when you first discovered or developed your high level of adaptability?"

"I'm going to have to think about that one a bit," said Mike.

The two men began silently walking toward the locker room.

"You know what," said Mike, "I think it was my junior year of high school when I wrecked my knee and ended my football career. My two big brothers were college stars, and I had always seen myself as following in their footsteps, and in a split second, all that was gone. I lost my girlfriend, some of my friends . . . I felt like just giving up. I got really angry, and then one day, I just decided to take back my life. I ran for student-body president and poured all my energy into that—and I learned maybe the most important lesson in my life: You just gotta adapt."

"So you see," Joe said, opening the locker-room door, "You already know about bounce."

"I do?"

"Sure, the story you just told me is the story of a bounce."

They entered the locker room, and Joe stopped in front of a mirror that was fogged from the moisture of the steam room. With his index finger he drew a large asymmetrical V on the mirror:

REINTEGRATION

DISINTEGRATION

Joe looked Mike in the eye. "People discover or develop their most important qualities when times get tough. That torn ligament of yours was a sudden loss of altitude for your life," he said, moving his hand down the left side of the V. "From the sound of things, your life kind of *disintegrated* for a while—lost your girlfriend, some of your friends, lost your dreams."

"Yeah, I guess disintegration is a good word for it," said Mike.

"But at some point, you hit the bottom," Joe continued, "and then you *reintegrated* around some new idea of yourself, and that idea included a really important quality—adaptability." As he said this, he traced the rising right side of the V. "Notice, the right-hand side is higher—reflecting that you actually end up stronger than when you began. That's why I said that your company is on the way to greatness, because with every sudden loss of altitude, there's the opportunity to learn to bounce."

"Tough times are the only times when people or teams get to discover their bounce," Joe continued. "In the army, I was a ranger. What's the first thing that comes to mind when you think of a ranger?"

"Tough as nails," said Mike.

"And do you think rangers are born tough or made tough?" asked Joe.

"I don't know, born tough, I guess."

"Wrong. Rangers are made, not born—and the making of a ranger begins way back at basic training. When a young recruit pulls up to the gate at Fort Benning in Georgia to report for basic training, he is stepping into a *disintegration machine,* and he has no idea what a drastic drop in altitude the army has in store for him. Basic training is all about breaking people down—it's really a highly controlled process of disintegration. The first step in building a great soldier is to first tear him down, just as the first step in your developing your adaptability was your torn ligament. Then the army builds recruits back up—it *reintegrates* them—combining their best as individuals with centuries-old knowledge of what makes a great soldier. And it doesn't stop there—every time a soldier wants to move up in the army, the army has a tougher disintegration experience waiting for him. Ranger school makes basic training seem like a Sunday picnic." He wrote the words and drew another V on the mirror.

RANGER

SOLDIER

RECRUIT

"It's always the same story: Disintegrate, then reintegrate."

Mike stared at the mirror as the lines and words began to blur. It sure *felt* as though his company was disintegrating. Were there things he and his team were about to learn about the company, its customers, and its markets that would make it stronger in the future? Things far more valuable than their quarterly sales performance? Did his company have still-hidden qualities—like his own personal quality of adaptability—that it was about to discover and develop? For the first time in weeks, he felt a flash of hope and excitement. But as Joe passed him on the way out of the locker room, Mike called out: "Hey, Joe, what makes you so sure that my company is not just going to keep right on disintegrating?"

Joe turned and smiled. "I said it sounds like your company is on the *road* to greatness. Only you will decide whether or not you take that road. It will depend on whether you learn to bounce. In any event, you never want to waste a perfectly good loss of altitude."

losing altitude

ny feelings of hope and excitement from the night before were gone by the time Mike pulled up to the office early the next morning. He was disappointed with Bill, his VP of operations, for resigning at the worst possible time.

Really wished he would have talked to me first, he thought, *not just left a note on my desk.*

Now everyone was going to be upset about Bill's leaving at the very time when they needed to be focused on turning the business around.

It was still dark outside when Mike set his laptop bag inside the door of his office and headed down to Bill's office. As he walked in, Bill looked up and Mike noticed something he hadn't seen before. Bill's face was tired and ashen—he looked beaten.

"Bill, I was surprised to get your letter," Mike began, trying to sound friendly.

Bill's face flushed. "I'm sorry, Mike. I just can't take the pressure anymore."

"I just wish you would have come to me about this," Mike said, tapping his fingers on the desk. Bill sank down in his chair.

"I'm really sorry, Mike, but I'm sixty-one years old, and I've been working eighty hours a week for almost a year now. I just can't keep up the pace anymore. My doctor tells me that if I don't do something different, I'll drop dead of a heart attack."

Mike felt the anger drain out of him. No one had done more for this company than Bill, and now it was clear that the pressures of the last year had burned him out. Mike plopped down in the chair next to Bill's desk.

"I know it's been a grind, Bill—and I understand where you're coming from. Can you give me twenty-four hours to think about it?"

Bill looked stricken. "Suuuuure," he said, ". . . but, Mike, I already told some of the team."

Mike's frustration leaked out. "Ah, Bill, I really wish you had waited."

Mike was still frustrated as he sat in the conference room waiting for his executive team to arrive for the 7:30 staff meeting. By now everyone in the company was probably buzzing about Bill's departure. Bill had robbed him of the ability to control the message, and he worried that some people would overreact.

IT Director Sean Tinsley was the first to arrive, and he slipped into a seat at the far end of the conference room and fiddled with his eyeglasses, repeatedly taking them off, bending the frame slightly, and putting them back on. Mike looked up and saw that the left side of Sean's glasses was jutting upward awkwardly. He smiled and continued doodling on his pad. The others filed in just before 7:30, Finance Director Paula Michaels, Sales VP Bob Fraley, and Bill, who didn't look at Mike when he walked in.

"How'd it go yesterday with Altech?" Bob asked, trying to break the tension.

"Brutal," grunted Mike, barely looking up from his pad. "If we screw up one more time, we're dead." The tension in the room eased slightly as people realized that Mike had apparently turned things around with one of their most important clients. Altech represented 5 percent of their total business, and a loss like that in such a tough economy would be devastating. Mike looked down at his pad and thought about his conversation with Joe Nicks the night before. *You never want to waste a perfectly good loss of altitude.* Right now he wasn't worried about wasting a loss of altitude, he was worried about a loss of altitude wasting *him*.

He looked around the table. "Folks, I don't need to tell

you that we are in a crisis here," Mike began. He felt the room snap to attention. "Our industry is being battered like never before, and there are no signs of a letup. And now corporate wants us to cut expenses ten percent."

"But, but we've already cut deep," Bill stammered. Mike shot him a glance.

"Well, Bill, it is what it is."

Bill's face flushed.

"And folks," Mike continued, "if we don't get a handle on our customer satisfaction problems, we may be faced with cutting even *more*. As most of you know, we almost lost the Altech account over disappointment with our products . . . but I did get to visit beautiful Omaha in December," he said, trying to lighten the mood a bit. He stopped and looked around the room.

"At times like these, we need to be willing to do things we wouldn't normally do. Now, who has some ideas on where we can cut costs?" The room was silent; they all looked at their hands. Paula scribbled furiously on her pad.

"You know, corporate really doesn't care how deep we cut last time, all they care about is that we cut again . . . and we are going to—" Suddenly the door opened and Mike's assistant, Susan, slipped in and walked to the far end of the conference room where Mike was sitting. She leaned over, and slipped him a note, and winced as she said, "I thought you'd want to see this."

wear your kevlar

mike sat back in his chair, staring at the table and feeling his heartbeat in his temples. The clock on the wall clicked off the seconds.

"Altech pulled the plug," he said finally, and then again

fell silent. He snapped his notebook shut and stood up. "Look, I don't like these corporate cost mandates any more than you do, but we are going to have to do what we need to. I'd like you all to come up with plans to reduce your departmental costs by fifteen percent," he said.

"I thought you said we only had to cut ten percent," Bill said sheepishly.

"You are going to replace the Altech account over the weekend, Bill?" Mike snapped. He immediately regretted the comment. "Our plans need to reflect the loss of the Altech business."

Back at his office, Mike placed a call to the Altech CEO that he was fairly sure wouldn't be returned. He began to weed through the more than three hundred e-mails that had collected over the past couple of days, until it was time to jump on a conference call with all the subsidiary general managers and his boss, Rachel, the parent company CEO.

"It's time for everyone to step up," said Rachel as she opened the meeting. Mike hit the speaker-phone button and pressed mute so that the others on the call wouldn't hear him as he continued to go through his e-mail. He viewed the call as largely a waste of time, but at least he was able to drag all of his e-mails that needed immediate action into a file and start working his way through them. Just whittling down the number made him feel a bit better—so he ate lunch at his desk.

He was running some scenarios in Excel when his cell phone chimed.

Dec 5, 3:32 PM

J Need someone to humiliate you in racquetball tonight?

Mike thumbed a response:

With the day I've had, you better wear your Kevlar. 9:30? M

Within seconds the cell phone chimed again.

Dec 5, 3:34 PM

J HOOAH. 9:30 it is.

Mike spent the rest of the afternoon lost in an Excel alternate universe. No matter how he ran the numbers, he couldn't figure out how to get another 15 percent of expenses out of the business. His neck and shoulders ached from leaning forward in his chair, and his eyes burned in an LCD screen haze. He glanced up at the clock—5:45, time to head for home—when he noticed Sean Tinsley standing in his doorway, his glasses still a bit crooked.

"Hey, what's up?" Mike asked, snapping his laptop shut.

"I heard about Bill." Sean began slowly.

"Yeah, I'm sorry we are losing him," Mike said as he bent over to slip his laptop into his computer bag.

"What are we going to do?" asked Sean.

"We?" responded Mike, a little too impatiently. "Sean, you keep providing leadership to the IT group, just like you have. I'll figure something out on the Bill situation, OK?" Sean shifted nervously in the doorway, but stood his ground. "Something else?" Mike asked, moving toward the door.

Sean cleared his throat. "Have you thought about Sally?"

"Have I thought what about Sally?" Mike grabbed his coat from the hook on the back of the door, and Sean moved sideways to let him pass.

"I think Sally could do Bill's job," said Sean as he followed Mike out the door and down the hall.

"Sally's a great person, and she does a terrific job with the second shift, but I'm not sure she's ready to run the whole operation. Has she even finished college?"

They had reached the front lobby when Sean stopped. "I don't know about that, Mike, but spend some time on the floor next week. I think you might see something special in Sally," he said.

Mike pushed out the glass doors and trudged through eight inches of new snow.

getting people right

at home, Mike played Wii Tennis with his daughters, but his mind was still at the office. He was quiet during dinner; his wife, Mary, realized that something must have happened today at work. After tucking the kids into bed, he kissed her. "Honey, I need to go to the gym and blow off some steam if I'm going to be of any use to you and the kids this weekend." Anger flashed in her eyes and she pulled away from him.

"You're gone all week every week, and then you come home and you're not really here!" she snapped. Mike looked down at the floor. She suddenly stepped forward and laid her head against his chest, then pulled away again and slipped down the hall.

Joe was already warming up on the court when he arrived at the gym. As Mike closed the glass door behind him, Joe tossed him the ball and grinned.

"Want a little warm-up before your whippin'?"

Mike slammed the ball hard against the front wall at a perfect angle. It sailed toward the back left corner and sent

Joe crashing into the side wall in pursuit. "Well, we *did* have a tough day, didn't we?"

Mike and Joe pounded away at the ball on the court. The soles of their shoes screeched, and sweat poured down their arms and legs and soaked their clothes. Near the end of a tough thirty-minute first game, Mike picked up a hand towel and tore off a strip to make a headband that would keep the sweat from running down into his goggles. Joe won the game 15–14.

In the second game, Joe jumped out to a six-point lead. But Mike came roaring back, scoring seven straight points to take the lead and finally win, 15–14, after forty-five brutal minutes. It was 10–10 in the tiebreaker when Joe hit a weak serve to Mike's forehand. Mike drew back with relish and smacked the ball as hard as he could in Joe's direction, hoping to jam him up on his return shot. Just then, Joe turned around and the ball smacked him square in the nose. Mike was mortified. Joe fell on the ground laughing, his nose bleeding profusely.

"Joe, I am so sorry!" Mike said. Joe laughed louder. "Are you OK?"

Now Joe was laughing to the point of tears. He sat up and pulled his hand from his nose—it made an odd dogleg left on the previously straight fairway of his face.

"I think it's broken!" exclaimed Mike. "I'll get you some ice."

The two of them sat on the court, Joe holding his head back with the ice wrapped in a towel, laughing every time Mike would say something. The towel had a bright red spot by the time Joe's nose stopped bleeding. He set it down beside him and leaned against the wall.

"How's your company doing with its bounce?" he asked.

Mike looked up, but quickly looked away, stinging with guilt at the sight of Joe's now crooked face.

"Not so good," he said. "I think our company is going to be a dead-cat-bounce sort of place."

"Why do you say that?" asked Joe.

"I don't know. To be honest, I don't think I have the right people on my team."

"Maybe they're afraid you're going to frag them," Joe said, laughing.

"Frag? What's that?"

"Frag . . . you know, injuring one of your own guys," he said, smiling and pointing to the huge purple welt that used to be his nose. Mike blushed.

Joe picked up the ice and put it on the bridge of his nose again. "It's always been interesting to me how you business guys always talk about getting the *right people*," he said, his voice muffled through the towel. "Seems to me, people in business are too concerned with getting the right people when they should be concerned with getting the *people right*."

"What do you mean?" Mike asked.

Joe put the ice back down on the floor and crossed his ankles in front of him. "When I was twenty years old with only a high-school education, the army put me in charge of a million-dollar piece of equipment, an M1 tank that could do tens of millions of dollars of damage. When I became a ranger, I was calling in air strikes by fifty-million-dollar aircraft that dropped bombs that cost a million apiece. The army takes thousands of kids like me and entrusts them with billions of dollars of technology and equipment—and the army has confidence that they will be able to make the toughest decision a human being can ever make—the decision of life or death for another human being. How is it that a bunch of blue-collar kids like me operate effectively in one of the most complex and stressful environments possible? The army does it by focusing ten percent of the effort on getting the *right people,* and ninety percent of the effort on getting the *people right.*"

Mike stared at Joe's comically swelling nose. "So how do you get the people right?"

"First," said Joe, "you have to understand why they do the things they do. You are obviously pretty frustrated by your team right now. What is it they are doing that has you so mad?"

Mike felt the tension returning to his back and shoulders. He scooted forward and lay down on his back.

"We are facing some really tough challenges right now, and they need to be in the game, you know what I mean? And instead, they are all diving under their desks. They just can't handle the stress—in fact, our VP of operations just up and quit today—after the company invested twelve years in him."

run to the sound of gunfire

Joe stood up and picked up his bloody towel.

"Let's go get something to drink." He tossed some quarters in the vending machine in the gym's deserted snack bar and brought two bottles of water over to a table.

"What would you do if some guy walked through that front door right now with a gun and started shooting?" he asked Mike, looking him straight in the eye.

Mike shifted uneasily. "I don't know. Run, I guess."

"That's exactly what you would do," Joe said, "and as a result of that, you'd be dead. The easiest target to hit is one running away from you—if he was any good, the guy with the gun would kill you before you made it three steps. You'd run because that's what humans instinctively do when they are threatened—and eons ago, back on the savanna, before there were such things as AK-47s, that worked fine. But with today's technology, running is a death sentence. What they teach you in basic training is not to run. If a gunman walked in that door right now, you'd see me dive behind that vending machine. Because if he isn't carrying anything bigger than, say, a nine-millimeter pistol, it might protect me long enough to figure out some way to survive.

"What you want your people to do—I didn't learn this until I got into ranger school—you want your people to run *to* the sound of gunfire, and that requires a person to go against every natural human urge."

"But why would you run *toward* gunfire?" asked Mike, drawing his chair up to the table.

"Because when you take cover, you only *think* you're safe. What you are really is stationary—and if your enemies are not stationary, they'll quickly surround you and find a weak point. So even though it seems counterintuitive, running toward the sound of gunfire is actually the safest thing you can do. To attack—to run to the sound of gunfire—is the only way to get your enemy to stop shooting at you for good. It's true in battle and it's true in life—attack your problems, attack what's a threat to you. It's just hard to get people to do it when the pressure's on, because they have to go against their natural tendencies."

"So how do I get my people to run to the sound of gunfire?" asked Mike.

"Oh, so you want to skip the whole basic training thing and go right to ranger school, huh?" laughed Joe.

"OK, so what would be basic training for my team?"

"It's all about the bounce, Mike," Joe said, taking a swig from his water bottle. "From the sound of things, your company is still in the disintegration stage. So you have to have a deep understanding of what's going on in your people. With that, you can start basic training."

"Well, I think I know what's going on inside them," Mike said. "They're completely freaked out."

"Probably right," said Joe. "People tend to get pretty anxious when they are disintegrating. The best thing you can do is to absorb anxiety."

"What do you mean *absorb anxiety?*"

"Just what I said. *Absorb the anxiety.* On a scale of one to ten, what's the anxiety level of your direct reports?"

"I don't know . . . nine," said Mike.

"OK," said Joe, "so your job over the next week should be to absorb enough anxiety for that level to go down to, say, a six."

"But just how does a person absorb anxiety?"

Joe glanced up at the clock on the wall. "Ouch, eleven thirty—Jennie's going to kill me. If you spend some time thinking about it, you'll come up with lots of ways—but Tom Hanks can get you started."

"Tom Hanks? The movie star Tom Hanks?" Mike asked.

"That's the guy," Joe said with a smile and stood up. "Watch the movie *Saving Private Ryan.* There's lots of stuff in there about absorbing anxiety," he said, heading for the door.

In the locker room, Mike stepped into the shower and turned the dial up as hot as he could stand it. *Absorb anxiety* . . . he stood thinking for a long time as steam filled the room.

Mary and the girls were fast asleep when he got home. He wasn't sleepy at all, so he went into the den, opened the door to the entertainment center, and rummaged through the family's DVD collection until he found *Saving Private Ryan.* He slid the DVD into the player and plopped down on the couch with the remote. In the early minutes of the movie, Mike remembered how much he had loved the film when he and Mary had seen it at the theater. It was heroism personified. About twenty minutes into the film, Mike suddenly sat forward as a scene unfolded: Tom Hanks, playing Captain Miller, was leading his troops over a hill on what they all knew was likely a suicide mission. They were charged with slipping behind enemy lines, finding a private named Ryan, and returning him back across the Allied lines to safety. As the troops humped over the hill, they were complaining about being sent on what they saw to be a nearly impossible, stupid mission. "So, Captain," shouted one of the grunts. "What about you? You don't gripe at all?" Captain Miller's response sent a chill down Mike's spine:

I don't gripe to you, Reiben. I'm a captain. There's a
chain of command. Gripes go up the chain, not down.
Always up. You gripe to me. I gripe to my superior
officer, so on, so on, and so on. I don't gripe to you.
I don't gripe in front of you. You should know that as
a ranger.

Gripes go up the chain of command . . . Mike pressed pause
on the remote and laid back on the couch, massaging the
stiff cords in the back of his neck. *I've been complaining to
my troops,* he thought sadly. *Not only have I not been absorbing anxiety, I've been creating it.* He shuffled up the stairs
to the bedroom and undressed silently. The silk of Mary's
nightgown and the warmth of her skin revived his spirits a
bit, but then she pulled away, leaving him alone on his side
of the bed. Lying beside her, listening to her breathe, his
determination grew. *I'm going to figure out how to get this
business to bounce,* he thought, *and I'll soak up every ounce of
anxiety in the whole company if that's what it takes.*

an absorbing morning

ike was the first into the office Monday morning. *I have no idea how I am going to get us out of this jam,* he thought, *but at least now I have something to focus on.* He erased some figures from the whiteboard behind his desk and wrote two letters in the center of the board:

A A

Absorbing anxiety was something that didn't come naturally to Mike, and he was going to need all the reminders he could get.

He dug through his e-mail until about six forty-five A.M., about the time he knew his boss, Rachel, would be arriving in the office. He picked up the phone and took a deep breath before dialing her direct line. When she answered, he began: "Rachel, this is Mike Maloney. Listen, I know you wanted our expense cuts by tomorrow, but I am calling to ask for a one-week extension."

"Mike, all the other subsidiaries have committed to get us numbers on time, and I need to get the final analysis done before the board meeting on the nineteenth—it's just not possible."

"I appreciate your situation, Rachel, and I don't want to do anything to hurt your ability to get stuff to the board with plenty of notice. But I really believe an extra week for my team would make the difference between a plan that merely stanches the bleeding and a plan that turns things around."

"Your numbers shouldn't be a surprise to you—your division has been deteriorating for more than a year. I can't believe you are just now getting around to asking these questions!"

Mike took a deep breath. "Rachel, I am asking for your support here. I won't let you down." The line went silent.

"OK, you've got a week. But if the finance people ask you to fly up here and pull an all-nighter to get me what I need, I expect you to do it."

"Done," said Mike. "Tell the bean counters I'll even bring the pizza."

"If they knew you called them bean counters, they'd give you a deadline of yesterday," she replied.

Just as he was hanging up the phone, Mike heard Bill unlocking his office door. He looked at his watch: 6:55 A.M. *Even after the guy has submitted his resignation, he is the first guy here and the last guy to leave,* thought Mike. He ambled down to Bill's office and stuck his head in the door. "Can I grab a few minutes, or do you want some time to get to e-mail first?" he asked.

"No, this is fine," Bill said, nervously clicking his ball-point pen. Mike dropped into the chair beside Bill's desk.

"Look, Bill, I didn't handle our discussion very well on Friday. Frankly, I was in a state of shock. You've been a rock for this company for so many years—I guess I was having a hard time imagining this place without you."

Bill exhaled loudly. "I'm having a really tough time imagining it myself."

Mike looked up. "What do you mean?"

"I don't want to leave the company. This place has been my life," said Bill sadly.

"Then why?" asked Mike.

"You just don't understand, Mike. . . . I've got some things . . . some things going on at home . . . I can't really go into it. If I keep putting in these hours, I could lose my family."

Mike sat back in the chair, stunned. It had never occurred to him that Bill might be quitting because of personal reasons. Sure, that's what he said in his resignation letter, but isn't that what everyone says when they resign? *Might lose his family . . . what could it be?* The thought of losing Mary and the girls made Mike shudder.

"What are you going to do?"

A look of pain crossed Bill's face. "I don't really know, Mike. I'm sixty-one years old, not the perfect age to go job hopping, huh? But I have got to find something where I can put in forty or fifty hours a week and still have the time to support a member of my family who really needs me."

"We need to figure out a way to make this company that place for you," Mike blurted out, not even sure what he was saying.

"Mike, my job is an eighty-hour-a-week job, even for someone who knows the business. There's no way I could do it and do what I need to do in my personal life."

Mike stood up and began pacing the floor.

"OK, so you can't do the VP job and have the personal time you need, . . . so let's figure out how the company can keep the benefit of your knowledge and experience, and most important, Bill, your strength of character. That's what we depend upon more than anything!"

All of a sudden, Bill looked totally different. Color rushed to his face and his eyes brightened. Then, after a moment, he seemed to deflate. "Mike, it's really nice of you to think this way, but this business is in crisis; it needs to be cutting costs aggressively—not finding ways to keep old guys like me on the payroll."

Mike looked out the window of Bill's office as people streamed into the office and the atrium began to spring to life. "You're right, Bill, it has to be something that's good for the company but still meets your needs. I think we can come up with something if we work together."

Bill's face brightened again. "I thought for sure you were going to beat on me to stay till we get through this rough patch."

"That would be my normal style, wouldn't it?" Mike said, smiling. Bill flashed an uncharacteristic grin.

"OK, so let's both sleep on it," Mike said, "but the main thing—I need to find your replacement and get some of the pressure off you as soon as possible. Do you know anyone who could do the job?"

"I'm not saying this to be egotistical, but you are going to have a hard time finding someone outside the company who understands all the different technologies and processes we use. We're a bit of an odd bird in the industry that way," Bill said.

Mike sat back down, and began tapping the armrests of the chair. "What about somebody from inside the company?"

Bill looked startled. "You mean you'd actually consider one of our own people to take my job?"

"Sure, if he's qualified," responded Mike.

Bill smiled again. "Well *he* is not qualified, but *she* just might be."

"What are you getting at?" asked Mike.

"Sally," Bill replied calmly. "She has done an amazing job with second shift, and she is one of the sharpest operations people I have ever known. She's green, Mike, but she could pull it off."

Sally again, thought Mike, *maybe Sean was on to something. Come to think of it, second shift always had the best production numbers. And it was second shift that had done the pilots for both the new quality program and the lean program.*

i want *your* job

back at the office, Mike clicked on the company phone directory and found Sally's cell-phone number. She wasn't due in till 3:00 P.M., but maybe he could catch her earlier. He sent her a text.

Minutes later came her reply:

> Sally, I'd like to grab a few minutes with you before you start your shift— any chance you are free for lunch?
>
> M

Mike spotted it immediately. *Anxiety.* She knows the

Dec 8, 7:47 AM

> S   Sure Mike. Everything OK?

company is going to go into cost-cutting mode, has probably heard that Bill is leaving, and may even be worried that second shift may be on the block. *Time to go into anxiety-absorption mode.*

> Everything is great, Sally, just blown away by 2nd shift numbers and want to learn more on how you are doing it. Noon—Pier View Grill?

M

Sally was waiting for him at the table when Mike arrived at the Pier View. It was the first time the two had sat down away from the office—one of only a handful of times they had met one-on-one. As they chatted, Mike became aware that Sally was a real powerhouse. She had on a crisp business suit—a marked difference from the white lab coat and clean-room hairnet Mike had always seen her in before. Over lunch, Mike learned that she was the mother of two young children and that although she had not yet finished her degree, she had been putting herself through night school and had only one semester remaining. She was married to a technical writer who worked from home and was able to spend lots of time with their children.

"Where do you see yourself going in life?" Mike asked. "What are your career goals?"

"Isn't it obvious, Mike?" she responded. "I want *your* job."

Mike was sold. He chuckled. "Are you willing to make a stop or two along the way?"

Sally smiled. "If I must."

"What I'm saying, Sally, is that I'd like you to take Bill's job."

A look of horror crossed her face. "No, Mike. Bill is my mentor. You'll never find anyone with his abilities. This business simply wouldn't survive without Bill."

Mike pushed his chair away from the table and crossed his legs. Apparently she didn't know. "Sally, I'm captain of the Bill fan club myself, but he is looking to downshift. He's at a stage in his life when the job just doesn't work for him anymore."

Sally leaned forward. "So Bill *wants* to leave his job?"

"That's right, and when I asked him who could replace him, he said you were the only person for the job." Sally sat back, stunned.

"You are asking me . . . you are offering . . . you want me to be vice president?"

"That's what I've been trying to tell you—if you just let me get it out." Mike said, smiling broadly.

"Yes, yes, yes!" she said, a little too loudly. People at the nearby tables turned and looked at her, and she blushed crimson.

a different kind of AA meeting

ike hadn't been to his office for more than ten minutes all morning, so he was eager to get to his desk and return calls and e-mails. But within minutes of getting back, he looked up to see his finance director, Paula, a witty African American woman in her fifties standing in his doorway, her reading glasses pulled down on her nose. She stared at the whiteboard:

$$A \quad A$$

"Don't tell me things have gotten so tight that we are renting out your office for Alcoholics Anonymous meetings." she smirked.

Mike broke into laughter. "No, just something I've been thinking about." *It's working,* he thought, *I'm being reminded to absorb anxiety.* "What's up?"

Paula walked toward Mike's desk, holding out a CD. "We all met over the weekend to identify the fifteen percent cost cuts, and I have combined them here into one spreadsheet. I've also told everyone to be on call to meet with you when you are ready to go over it."

"How long were you guys here over the weekend?" asked Mike.

"About six hours on Saturday and four hours on Sunday," said Paula.

"I'm really sorry."

"What?"

"I'm sorry you guys had to spend so much time over the weekend," Mike said.

"It's no big deal. I know the people in corporate finance are pushing for this stuff . . . so you want me to call the meeting for four o'clock?" She tried to hand him the CD. Mike pushed his chair back and looked up.

"Before I look at that, tell me, how do you guys feel about the plan you put together?"

"Honestly?" She shifted nervously. "I guess it's OK given the circumstances. . . . I mean, you have to do what you have to do."

Mike stood up and looked out the window at the parking lot below. "Paula, you are one person around here I can really count on to say what you really think—what do you think is the consensus about the plan?"

"Well, . . ." she began, and then paused for a long time and looked out on the parking lot too, "to be honest, Mike, we are rearranging the deck chairs on the *Titanic* here.

There are some real critical strategic decisions that need to be made in our business. We are not making those decisions; we are just making cuts to make corporate happy. So the truth of the matter is, we've made some cuts, but we don't really have a plan."

Mike stood with his hands in his pockets staring out the window. "Then we are not making the cuts right now," he said.

"What? Mike, you don't understand. Corporate finance is breathing down my neck for these numbers—we've got to deliver them tomorrow! I mean, Rachel will have an absolute cow if you are late with this."

"I've already talked to Rachel, and she wants us to do what's right for the business," said Mike.

"You . . . talked to Rachel? And she . . . you're kidding. This does not sound like the Rachel I know."

"You let me handle Rachel, and if corporate finance calls you on this, transfer the call to me," said Mike.

Paula smiled. "I hope you have a can of pepper spray in your desk, 'cause you're going to need it."

Mike turned and looked her right in the eye. "Our job is to protect and grow this business, and sometimes we have to save the people at corporate from themselves. They are under a lot of pressure, and they are doing the best with the information they have—but in the end, we are the people they trust to protect this business, and the people and families who depend on it for their livelihood."

Paula was grinning from ear to ear. "What do you want me to tell the team?"

"Tell them first that I apologize that they spent their weekends trying to solve a puzzle without a vital piece that I am supposed to provide—a strategy. I mean it, I sincerely apologize. Tell them I appreciate the work they have done, and I am sure it will give us a lot of insights, but we are not going to be making cuts till we come up with a plan—and that they can count on me to work shoulder to shoulder with them to create that plan.

"Aye aye, sir!" Paula smiled, saluted, turned, and walked out the door.

late-night run with freddy krueger

 the next few days went by in a blur. Sally accepted the position of VP of operations and was a veritable whirlwind of activity. Every time Mike walked by the conference room, he saw her huddled with a different group of people. When Mike told Bill of his decision to make Sally VP, Bill asked if he might be considered for Sally's old job running second shift—he felt that it would be the perfect fit for his family situation. Mike told Bill he would consider it on two conditions: (1) Sally would make the final decision, and (2) Bill would be paid 20 percent more than the other shift managers, and for that, he would get up every morning and ask himself how to sow seeds of hope and confidence in the company. Mike decided a company can't have too many anxiety absorbers. Bill's response was that he always tried to build people up, and Mike replied "I know you do, Bill—you are our best at it—but I know if I pay you for it, you'll remember to do it even more." Bill left Mike's office beaming.

Still, Mike grew uneasy as the week wore on. Sure,

people seemed to be happier and more upbeat, but the fact of the matter was that his company was getting crushed in the marketplace, and the financials were beginning to hemorrhage. He was absorbing anxiety, but that wasn't going to turn the numbers around. He had only bought a week's delay, and the clock was ticking.

His gym clothes made the trip in the backseat of his car every day to and from work, but he just couldn't seem to find the time to break away. Finally, on Wednesday, he sent Joe a text:

> Need to run tonight bad. Balmy 21 deg. Want to get in 6 mi. or so? 9:30?

M

Joe's response came just minutes later:

Dec 9, 3:34 PM

> trying to dump some of that anxiety you've been absorbing? :) sure I'll help you wring it out. see you at the gym.

J

Mike went home and had dinner with the family, helped the girls with their homework, and then headed out for the gym.

The sight of Joe nearly knocked him down. The damage

from Mike's errant racquetball shot a few days ago was
now in full bloom on Joe's face. He had two black eyes, and
running down the bridge of Joe's nose, also purple, was a
piece of white medical tape anchored at the top and bottom
with a cross-strip of tape—forming a large white I in the
middle of his face. He looked as if he had been hit by a
truck, and yet there he stood, grinning that goofy grin of his.

"I can't believe I did that to you," Mike said, squinting
and shaking his head.

"You did me a favor!" Joe said, raising a defiant fist. "My
buddies from my old unit have this ongoing contest to see
who can get the sickest looking injuries. We take pictures of
them with our cell phones and send them around. My mug
is running at number two right now!"

"Who's number one?" asked Mike, not sure he wanted to
know.

"Dude fell off his snowboard last week. Broke his elbow.
His arm was pointing completely the wrong direction!"

"Nice," said Mike, wanting to change the subject.

They pushed out the front door of the gym in a jog,
crossed the parking lot, and fell into an easy rhythm in
the amber glow of the streetlights that lined the Charles
River. Their nylon jackets rustled to the beat of their feet
crunching through the now-crusty snow that had fallen
over the weekend. After a couple of miles, Mike felt his body
start to relax. He thought about Mary and the girls and the

time they had spent together in Cabo San Lucas during the girls' spring break. He thought of how great the sun had felt on his skin in the mornings; he remembered splashing with the girls in the surf for hours and the sweet taste of tequila in the margaritas he and Mary had enjoyed while watching the sun set that last night. Now those moments on the beach seemed a lifetime ago. He and Mary barely talked anymore, much less really enjoyed each other's company the way they used to. Ever since the family's move from Charlotte, there'd been a tension between them. She was having a tough time making friends in Boston, and Mike's constant business travel had made matters even worse. Mike could tell she resented him for moving the family away from a community they all loved and for taking a job that required so much from him. What was he doing here in Boston, with all this snow and ice? The family had loved Charlotte. Why hadn't he stayed with his old company?

Mike suddenly felt sad and helpless. Snow began to fall, and the two men continued around the park silently until Mike's pedometer began beeping.

"That's three miles. Head back toward the gym?" he asked, glancing in Joe's direction. The sight of him made Mike grin. Joe had the hood of his gray army sweatshirt pulled tight over a knit cap. The bruised upper face and perpendicular angles of tape across the middle made Joe look like some updated version of Freddy Krueger.

"What's so funny?" asked Joe.

"Sorry, Joe," Mike said, "but you look messed up."

"Badge of honor," Joe said, laughing. "Fragged by an MBA in a fancy suit."

They settled back into a quiet pace as they retraced their steps toward the gym. It was snowing hard now, and the wind had begun to blow in off the harbor. Mike adjusted his headband down over his ears and pulled up his hood. He snuck a glance in Joe's direction. Joe's powerful body glided effortlessly. His breathing was relaxed for having just run three miles. Then Mike noticed something—except for his forward motion on the street, Joe barely moved. His chin was tucked down into his neck and his shoulders didn't seem to rise or fall at all. He was only five ten. Mike was an easy three inches taller, but he found himself lengthening his gait to keep up.

Mike wondered what Joe's life was like as a ranger in Afghanistan. He imagined him in hard pursuit of the Taliban, riding shotgun in a Humvee, or scaling one of the vertigo-inducing peaks he had seen on news reports. *Had Joe ever killed anyone?* Mike wondered. Try as he might, Mike had a hard time picturing his happy-go-lucky friend hunkered down in some ravine gravely facing a life-or-death situation.

The more Mike thought about Joe, running quietly beside him, the more frustrated he became with the issues he was facing back at the office. Suddenly, he felt silly taking advice from a guy who was eight years younger, who had probably never even had a job in business. Sure, more of his team members seemed to have their heads in the game. But the company was facing huge problems, and those problems weren't going to go away just because a few people had had their anxiety absorbed. *I've recklessly used political capital with Rachel asking for that extension,* Mike thought. *Now she's going to see me as weak. I should have just submitted the cuts when she asked me for them.* Mike was getting angry. Joe had led him down the primrose path with his theories about bounces and absorbing anxiety—and in the meantime, the business continued to crater.

"Joe, mind if I ask you a question?" Mike asked when they were just a few blocks away from the gym.

"Shoot, Bro," Joe responded.

It's 2009, Mike thought. *Who still calls people Bro?* "I've been thinking about some of the things you said," he began, "and it seems like some of your ideas just don't line up." Joe stared straight ahead silently. "You said something like a crisis is a terrible thing to waste, because people are willing to do things they wouldn't normally do, right?"

"Yeah," said Joe, still not turning to look at Mike.

"Well, it seems to me that the one thing that exists in a crisis that doesn't exist in normal times is pressure, right?"

"Sounds right," Joe shot back.

"So here's what doesn't make sense to me," Mike said, convinced he had led Joe into a trap of his own making. "Why do you want to take the pressure *off* people in a crisis? Don't you really want them to feel the heat—so that they'll do these things they *supposedly* are willing to do only in tough times?" Mike immediately regretted he had let his sarcasm slip out.

Still gliding forward effortlessly, Joe turned and looked at Mike. "I never said to take the pressure off people, Mike. I said absorb the anxiety."

"Seems like the same thing," said Mike impatiently.

two types of anxiety

They had arrived at the front entrance of the gym, but neither of them reached for the door. They both stood shifting from foot to foot, their faces slashed with colors from the health club's neon sign above.

"Not the same thing at all," Joe said, looking up. "The military training I have been through involved some of the biggest pressures I have ever faced. The army knows that pressure always generates anxiety, so the army's training programs are built around making sure soldiers have the right *type* of anxiety."

"There are different *types* of anxiety?" asked Mike.

"Yep," replied Joe, grabbing the door handle and motioning him inside. They headed for the locker room.

"Most people live in a comfort zone," continued Joe. "It takes pressure to get people out of their comfort zone to change. Remember, any meaningful human change requires a bounce, and bouncing is painful. As the heat is turned up, disintegration starts, and people naturally start to feel anxious. Let's call it Anxiety 1—the fear of change. When people feel Anxiety 1, they tend to cling to the things that got them through hard times in the past. The problem is, those things may not get them through the new challenge. Basic training is an engineered crisis. You get these young kids coming in, and the drill sergeant starts, well, *drilling* them."

Joe smiled and Mike chuckled. "These kids start feeling anxious, and pretty soon they are doing things they did in high school when they felt anxious—flapping their jaws, complaining, withdrawing, or blaming the army or the other guys in the squad. The fear of change, Anxiety 1, gets 'em doing all these things. Problem is, on the battlefield, those things will turn them and their buddies into a pink mist. The army knows this. So it tries to make sure, in training soldiers, that Anxiety 2 always exceeds Anxiety 1."

"What the hell is Anxiety 2?" Mike asked, grabbing a towel from the bin.

Joe sat down on the bench and started untying his shoes. "Anxiety 1 is the fear of change," answered Joe. "Anxiety 2 is the fear of what will happen to you if you don't change."

"So why didn't you tell me about this Anxiety 2 before?" Mike asked. "Why all this talk about 'absorbing anxiety'?"

Joe stopped untying his shoes and looked up. "Because at the beginning of disintegration, there's usually so much anxiety around that it all feels the same to people—they can't tell the difference between Anxiety 1 and Anxiety

2. Once you get a person's Anxiety 1 down a bit, you have a chance to get them to see that they have *options*— that they have *control* over some important part of the situation. Only then are they going to really disintegrate and reintegrate in an effective way. The job of a leader is to convert Anxiety 1 to Anxiety 2."

"But how do you do that?" Mike asked.

"By showing them what they can do about the situation," Joe replied.

"But I'm not sure these people really *can* do anything about our situation," said Mike slowly.

"Then you are definitely screwed," replied Joe, shaking his head.

Mike drove home thinking about what Joe had said. When he opened the door from the garage, he saw Mary sitting at the kitchen table, a glass of red wine in front of her. As he moved closer he could see that her makeup was smeared— she'd been crying. He sat down beside her and took her hands in his. Her eyes welled with tears and Mike looked down at the table. They sat there silently for a long time.

"I just can't do this anymore." Mary finally began, choking back the tears.

"Can't do what?" he asked, looking up.

"Can't do this marriage," she said quietly, tears now streaming down her face.

Mike felt like he'd been punched in the gut. His mouth opened, but no words came out. He felt the cold chill of fear and his head was spinning. *I could lose my family.*

"Mary, honey . . ." he finally stammered, "I know you're mad at me for moving us here . . ."

"How can you be so clueless?" she shouted, glancing up at the ceiling in fear she'd awoken the girls. She clenched her jaw and lowered her voice. "It has *nothing* to do with being mad or with the stupid move."

"Then what?" he asked, tears welling in his own eyes.

"I'm all alone here, Mike," she sobbed. "I'm lonely. You don't talk to me anymore. I know you're fighting battles at work, but you haven't made me a part of them. We're not a couple anymore, we're just two people sharing a mortgage."

Mike was stunned. *I can't lose my family, they're everything to me.* They sat there silently, not looking at each other, for several minutes.

"I feel like I'm falling apart," Mike blurted, "I've always had it all together . . . for the first time in my life I feel like I'm going to fail."

"Why haven't you talked to me?" Mary asked. She wiped a tear away.

"I guess I was just too ashamed of what I was feeling to talk to you about it. I'm sorry, Mary, I'm really sorry." Suddenly Mike felt the dam break—words began tumbling out. He told Mary about the company's deteriorating financial condition and about the constant pressure he was feeling from Rachel. He told her about losing the Altech account and about almost losing Bill because of the stress they were all under. He even told her about this army guy he'd met at the gym who believed that tough times like these could even be good for people, if they handled them right.

Mary scooted her chair over and threw her arms around him and they held each other for a long time. They sat at the table and talked into the early hours of the morning, talked like they hadn't talked in years. Mike found himself wondering how he'd allowed them to drift so far apart. But the more he shared, the more animated Mary became, eventually sharing some of her own recent challenges— how much she missed her friends and family in Charlotte and how worried she was that the girls might be having a difficult time adjusting to the new school.

It was past three when they finally went to bed. Exhausted, Mary fell right to sleep, and Mike lay looking at the ceiling, thinking: *If companies can bounce so can people and marriages.* Tonight, he and Mary had absorbed each other's anxiety. Never again would he shut his wife out. From now on, they were a team—they'd face life's challenges together.

christmas ornaments and oranges

When Mike walked into the conference room for the weekly staff meeting at 7:30 the next day, his team was already waiting for him. He looked around the table and smiled. "Let's all welcome Sally to her first executive staff meeting."

"Welcome to the lion's den," cracked Sales VP Bob Fraley, and the room burst into nervous laughter.

"I want to do something a bit different this meeting," Mike began. "I want to hear from each of you on how you think people in the company are feeling right now."

Dead silence. Several people looked down at the printed meeting agenda in front of them. More silence. "Anyone?" Mike let an uncomfortable silence go on for what seemed to most in the room like an hour.

Finally, Bill cleared his throat, and all eyes in the room darted toward him. His faced blushed bright red against his thinning white hair, just as it always did when he was getting ready to say something difficult. "Jeez, Mike, what do you think they are feeling? Our revenues have been flat or down two years in a row, we did a layoff just six months ago, and now we just lost the Altech contract. I'll tell you how people are feeling—they're thinking they are about to lose their jobs."

Another long silence. Everyone looked at Mike, bracing for his response—but Mike just looked thoughtfully at Bill. "Sounds like our folks are pretty anxious," he said finally. "Who's next?"

"The technology people are pretty much in the same place," said Sean. "They're spending a lot of time around the water cooler talking about where they think this is all going to end up."

"You know salespeople," added Bob from the other side of the table. "They're always the first to lose faith and the last to get it back. The loss of Altech has really shaken my team—I'm spending half of my time just talking guys down from the ledge."

"I'll be honest with you, Mike," added Paula after another long silence. "I've worked here for fifteen years—and in my job I am living with the numbers—and I can honestly say I have never been more concerned about the future of this company than I am right now, today."

Sally, the newest member of the executive team, sat quietly.

Mike stood up and put his hands in his pockets. "So we're in agreement," he said. "Anxiety at the company is at an all-time high. I feel it too. The question is, what should we do about it?" He walked over to the Christmas tree that was set up in the conference room and began absentmindedly flicking the glass ornaments. Suddenly he plucked one of the ornaments off the tree and smiled. He walked over to the conference table, held the ornament about shoulder high and dropped it on the floor. It shattered into a thousand pieces, startling everyone.

"That ornament just encountered a sudden loss of altitude," he said, "and it didn't work out so well." He walked around to where Sean Tinsley was sitting and picked up an orange that Sean had sitting in front of him. "Mind if I borrow this, Sean?"

"As long as you don't throw it at me," Sean replied. Sally giggled.

Mike held the orange about shoulder high and dropped it, and it landed with a thud. "Same loss of altitude, different result. Much less dramatic. Less damage—but still some damage—just all on the inside. But if I had one of those hard rubber balls in here and I dropped it from about the same height, it would bounce back almost as high as my hand."

Mike ran his fingers through his hair and paced to the far side of the conference room. "I think what is making people in the company so anxious right now is that they all know our company has encountered a sudden loss of altitude. And they are rightfully wondering whether the company is going to be like that Christmas ornament and shatter into a million pieces, or like that orange—get badly bruised—or if we are going to bounce back, like a rubber ball. And I guess, to a large extent, the answer to that question is up to us." Mike sat down in his chair and pushed himself back from the table. The room was silent except for the ticking of the clock.

warren buffett's swim trunks

m ike stood up again, went to the blackboard, and drew the bounce.

REINTEGRATION

DISINTEGRATION

"I have a friend who thinks that *losses of altitude* are simply a part of life," Mike began. "He thinks that people, companies, countries, they all go through difficult times . . . times that require them to face tough new facts, discard solutions that have worked in the past, and eventually remake themselves. He thinks that no matter who you are, this is a painful process that we all tend to resist—no matter how good our intentions are."

"Well, if we are really going to be honest with one another as a team," Bill said, flushing pink again, "we are going to have to admit to ourselves that we have been disintegrating for a couple of years now."

"Why do you say that, Bill?" asked Mike.

"Because we have not had our eye on the ball these last few years," said Bill. "We've delivered on most of our financial commitments to corporate, but in the marketplace, we have lost our edge. The growth in the markets we serve has disguised that fact, but now our market is down, and the reality is right there, staring us in the face."

"Reminds me of my favorite Warren Buffett quote," quipped Paula: "'It's only when the tide goes out that you find out who's not wearing swimming trunks.'"

"You saying we're standing naked in knee-deep water?" Bob chimed in.

Paula shot back, "In your case, Bob, that's a terrible thought to ponder." Everyone laughed.

"Bill's right," Bob said, jumping to his feet and startling everyone. "I don't want to sound like a broken record, but I have been saying for years that we just aren't leading our market in innovation, in knowledge of our customers—not like we used to."

"That's true, Bob," Paula said, raising her voice a bit. "You have been saying that, but what you always neglect to include in your speech is how we are going to pay for all that innovation and customer knowledge. The numbers

don't lie—we can barely fund the things we have going
on now. Your answer to every problem is to open a new
market, come up with a new product, give the customers
everything they ask for. We just can't afford all this. We've
tried it your way, and that's what has gotten us into this
mess." The room was heating up. Old resentments were
flowing back to the surface, old wounds reopening.

"Well, if our G and A expenses weren't ten percent of
revenue, maybe we would have money to invest in our
customers!" shouted Bob.

Mike thought back to what Joe had said about new
recruits facing the pressure of basic training. *They'll revert to
what they used to do, "flapping their jaws, complaining, withdrawing, or blaming the army or the other guys in the squad."*

The group is disintegrating, thought Mike, and he was
about to intervene. Then he thought, *Hey, maybe this is a
good thing.* Suddenly, the usually invisible Sean shouted
above the din, in a voice louder than appropriate, "You
know what the problem is?" Shocked, the whole room
turned and faced him, and then began to laugh. Sean,
embarrassed, quickly sat down and blushed.

"Go ahead, Sean. What is it?" said Mike quietly.

"It's that ridiculous corporate overhead rate. How do
they expect us to serve our clients when we are paying
so much in corporate overhead?"

The room went quiet again. Bill was the first to speak. "Sean, I appreciate your perspective, but let's be honest with ourselves here, OK, guys? If we want to blame someone, we should blame the people sitting around this table. We are the ones at fault."

Another long silence.

holding hands in traffic

"**I** don't think we should be looking for someone to blame," said Mike finally, "though I appreciate the great sense of responsibility you feel for the company, Bill—and I know you all feel. What I'd like us to be talking about is what determines whether our business, in tough times, is going to be like a Christmas ornament or an orange or a rubber ball."

Always the engineer, Sean blurted out, "Well, it's the physical structure of a sphere that determines its resilience. Technically, that's what the word *resilience* means—ability to bounce back. So I wonder if companies have a *resilience structure* just like objects have a physical structure."

"Right!" said Mike. "So here's what I'd like your help thinking about: If life is really just a series of disintegrations and reintegrations, how do we build a company that disintegrates and reintegrates really well? The question is not just how do we turn our business around; it is how do we improve our resilience structure, to use Sean's words?

What causes companies, or for that matter, people, to *bounce*?"

"Guys, we are talking like we have never bounced before!" said Bob suddenly. "Remember the downturn of 2001? Remember how terrible things looked for about twelve months? Everyone was predicting we wouldn't survive. Not only did we survive, we came roaring back and passed a lot of our competition. We know how to do this!"

"So what enabled the company to bounce back in 2002?" asked Mike.

"You know, we could make this a lot more difficult than it is," replied Bob. "The fact is, a lot of this stuff is mental. You make up your mind to do something, and finally you just find yourself doing it." Mike went to the board and wrote *MENTAL* right under the point of the bounce diagram.

"OK, so Bob is saying there is a real mental aspect to an effective bounce," said Mike. "How is the *thinking* in companies that bounce different than in those that don't?"

"Well, it seems to me you have to be willing and able to see things as they really are," said Bill. "I mean, there are probably a lot of companies out there in our market that are still in denial—or are caught up in nostalgia for the 'good old days.' It seems like today we're saying that we think the good old days in our business are gone. We either change, or we get run over." Under *MENTAL*, Mike wrote, *SEE REALITY CLEARLY.*

"You know, it's kind of weird," said Bill, "but here, we are saying for the first time that we are faced with a situation where we either change or die, and I actually feel *relieved.* I haven't been this hopeful in forever—and we haven't even talked about how we are going to get out of this mess." Joe's words rang in Mike's mind: *The job of a leader is to convert Anxiety 1 to Anxiety 2. The group was doing the conversion itself!*

"So what are some other aspects of the mental side of resilience, of bouncing back?" asked Mike, his excitement building.

"I think another key during a difficult time is to not go off half-cocked," said Sally, finally comfortable enough to wade into the discussion a bit. "A lot of times, when times get tough, people run around like the building is on fire. They end up treating the symptoms of problems and not the root causes. There's a saying I like: 'Don't just do something, stand there.' People would do well to think about that during tough times."

"That's great, Sally," said Mike and he went to the board again and wrote *TREAT CAUSES, NOT SYMPTOMS.*

"Another thing that's important in terms of mental issues," said Bill suddenly, "is . . . well, we need to remember that *we* are in control of how we respond to a situation. We can't blame outside forces, like corporate or the market or customers, for our problems." Mike wrote, *"WE CONTROL," NOT 'THEY CONTROL"* on the board.

"What else?" asked Mike.

Paula had been sitting quietly for a few minutes; suddenly she turned and faced the group. "We need to focus on attacking our problems and not one another."

No fragging, Mike thought to himself, trying hard not to crack a smile. Paula turned and faced Bob. "Bob, I owe you an apology. I was out of line a few minutes ago. Your job as head of sales is to advocate strongly for our customers, and if you ever stop doing that, we are in real trouble."

"Especially if I'm not wearing swim trunks," Bob said, smiling broadly. The room erupted.

"Sometimes the goals of the finance department and the sales department may be in conflict," Paula continued earnestly, "and at those times, we as a team have to hammer out the best solution. One of the things that my mom said to me when my sisters and I were kids was 'Hold hands in traffic.' I think that is good advice. Our company is in heavy traffic right now—we are in the middle of an eight-lane freeway—and above all, we need to remember to stick together." Mike wrote, *HOLD HANDS IN TRAFFIC*.

He stood back and reviewed what he had written.

REINTEGRATION

DISINTEGRATION

MENTAL

- *SEE REALITY CLEARLY.*
- *TREAT CAUSES, NOT SYMPTOMS (DON'T JUST DO SOMETHING; STAND THERE).*
- *"WE CONTROL," NOT "THEY CONTROL."*
- *HOLD HANDS IN TRAFFIC.*

He was copying his notes from the board onto his pad when Susan slipped into the conference room and motioned to him that his nine o'clock appointment was waiting for him. "I'll be there in ten," he whispered.

Looking around the table, he asked, "Where do you all want to go from here?" as he sat back down. It was the first time anyone remembered Mike being willing to be late for a meeting.

Sally cleared her throat and said, "I feel like we made some progress as a team here, but we are facing some real challenges, and we need to bring a sense of urgency to solving them. What if we all just cleared our calendars for the whole day Friday and locked ourselves in a room and attacked the issues." Everyone simultaneously began checking their BlackBerry calendars for their Friday schedules.

"I think it's a great idea," said Paula.

"Me too," added Sean and Bill in unison.

Bob looked up from his BlackBerry and said, "I'll have to step out from eleven to noon for a call with a big prospect—but Paula, I know you'll represent Sales for me in my absence." Everyone cracked up.

"So Friday, all day, it is." Mike said. He hadn't even looked at his calendar for Friday. Whatever was on his schedule, it wasn't as important. He finished copying the notes from the board onto his pad and sat for a moment and reflected on what had just happened. In a little more than an hour, his executive team had themselves converted their Anxiety 1 into Anxiety 2. He snapped his portfolio shut and hurried down the hall to meet with his nine o'clock.

a mission misstatement

ike couldn't wait to get to the gym and tell Joe about the staff meeting. He headed out right after work, dressed in the locker room, slipped his weight-training card into his portfolio and headed for the weight room. Joe hadn't arrived yet, so Mike did some stretching and rope jumping to warm up.

Joe walked into the room looking a lot better. The swelling in his nose had gone down quite a bit, and the bruising under his eyes had faded except for two blue-black crescents—making him look like a football player ready for a game. He had removed the long strip of tape down the bridge of his nose, leaving just the two white crossbeams. "You're actually starting to look human," said Mike, surveying Joe's face.

"Yeah, until you drop a forty-five-pound weight or something on my head tonight," said Joe.

"Watch your back," quipped Mike.

"Start with some bench press?" Joe asked, motioning toward the bench.

"Sure," replied Mike. Joe lifted from the rack a forty-five-pound plate with each hand and placed one on each side of the bar, then added two more forty-fives.

"Going light for your warm-up, are you?" Mike asked sarcastically. Joe just smiled, laid down on the bench, and began to exhale quickly in a loud *shish* sound. Mike moved into position to spot him, and Joe lifted the bar off the rack. Joe did ten quick reps, exhaling every time he pushed the bar from his chest. He sprang up, his face crimson and veins popping out of his neck. Mike slid the outer two forty-fives off the bar and replaced them with twenty-fives. "I don't want to show you up too early in the workout," he said, sitting down on the bench.

Joe feigned shock as he looked at each end of the bar. "I think you are looking for the women's gym, Madam," he said, taking up the spotter's position. Mike's arms and chest burned as he struggled to get off seven reps. On the seventh, Joe shouted, "One more, Bro!" and somehow Mike locked his elbows one more time. *Too many missed days at the gym,* thought Mike. *If I had gotten in here regularly these last few months, I'd be giving this guy a run for it.*

They did five sets of bench presses and then dropped some weight and did four sets of military presses. They then did four sets of flies and added two sets each of incline presses and decline presses while waiting for the squat rack to be available. Mike dutifully recorded the weight and total number of reps for each exercise.

"So how's it going at the salt mine?" asked Joe as he inhaled and tightened his weight belt down as tight as it would go. His waist shrank to what looked like twenty-five inches. He began stacking forty-fives on the bar. *This animal is going to squat 315 in his warm-up set!* Mike thought.

"Pretty good, actually," Mike said out loud. "I think we are actually beginning to make some progress."

"Hooah," Joe said, stepping under the bar, bending his knees slightly and jerking the bar up off the rack. The ends of the bar bent downward and the huge mass of iron swayed precariously from side to side. Mike reached up and put both hands next to the bar. Joe stabilized the bar and knocked out ten reps like nothing.

"So tell me about it," Joe said when he had caught his breath, stepping from foot to foot and shaking out his legs.

Mike told him the whole story, how at the staff meeting he had just asked a couple of simple questions and seen his management team transformed before his eyes as they themselves converted their Anxiety 1 to Anxiety 2. "We even talked about what it is that enables some companies to bounce while others just crash."

"Cool," said Joe. "What'd you come up with?" Mike flipped open his portfolio to the diagram he had copied from the board and turned it toward Joe.

"We think that there are mental factors that determine which companies bounce and which don't," said Mike, pointing to the word *MENTAL* and the points written underneath.

Joe glanced at the diagram and looked up. "Yeah, that makes sense," he began. "There is definitely a mental component to bounce—we call it *mental toughness* in the military." He cocked his head and was silent for a few seconds. "No doubt . . . you are on to something there." Mike nodded excitedly.

"So what else did you come up with?" asked Joe. "What else makes a company bounce?"

"I was hoping you might be able to help me figure that out," Mike said, pulling some weight off the bar, tightening up his own weight belt, and moving into position on the squat rack.

"Jeez, I just shoot people and blow stuff up. I haven't a clue about fancy corporate stuff. *You're* the suit, remember?" said Joe.

Mike struggled through six squats, watching himself in the mirror as his face was transformed into something alien-looking under the strain. After he finished his set, he wiped his face with a towel. "OK, so let's not talk about companies, let's talk about the army. What makes a ranger team bounce?"

Joe looked straight at Mike, his eyes burning with intensity. Several seconds passed in silence. "For a ranger, it's all about the mission."

"Mission, that's good," said Mike, rolling the idea around in his head. "We have missions in business too. We call it a mission statement."

"A mission *what?*" Joe shot back, wrinkling his nose.

"You know, a mission statement, a statement of what your purpose is," Mike said, feeling a little defensive.

"Your *purpose?*" Joe said, wrinkling his nose again.

"Sure," countered Mike, determined to give Joe a lesson in management. "For instance, our mission at CRX is: Help our clients reduce their costs and improve their performance by leveraging information technology."

Joe shot Mike a quizzical look. "No offense, but that sounds like a complete *crock.*"

"No, Joe, this is how businesses do missions," Mike said, a bit hesitantly. "A committee at our company spent six months coming up with that mission statement. It tells us what we ought to be doing in the company."

"Yeah, and how's that working for you?" Joe shot back. "Look, I don't mean to hurt your feelings or anything, but that sentence doesn't tell anyone jack about what they ought to be doing. And if you think about it, you know I'm right. You really don't know what the word *mission* means, do you?"

"Enlighten me," Mike said, now completely insulted.

"Now don't go off pouting like a marine," Joe said, "hear me out. To a soldier, everything is about the mission. Sometimes a mission is that we are going to take X hill by 0900 hours and hold it. To a soldier, a mission is something specific, something vital. If you fail on your mission, you know someone may die—maybe you, maybe one of your buddies. With everyone completely committed to the mission, we have the best chance of everyone coming out alive.

"The last mission my squad had in Afghanistan was trying to protect a little village out in the middle of nowhere. We'd come into town in the daytime and offer medical attention, help dig a sewer line, whatever. Then at night, the bad guys would come in, terrorize the townspeople, and kill anyone who they suspected had talked to us, and the next week, we'd come in and do it all again. Might seem hopeless to people on the outside. But to us, it was the mission—at that moment, the most important thing in our lives." He reached into his gym bag for his wallet and fished out a tiny snapshot. In it, Joe was standing in the middle smiling, surrounded by five smiling, waving Afghani youngsters. "We knew if we failed in our mission, these kids didn't have a chance," he said quietly.

"Commitment to a mission makes people bounce," Joe continued, after a long pause, "whether they're on a football field or in Afghanistan or in a business. It's everything. When you can tell me what hill you are going to take and how you are going to take it, then you'll know you have a mission. Not before. None of the people at your company are going to die if you fail at your mission, but they might lose their jobs. And except for losing a loved one, that feeling might be as close to death as a lot of stateside people get— this side of actually getting their ticket punched."

Mike's anger began to dissipate. Maybe Joe was right. Maybe the whole mission-statement thing in corporate America was an attempt to capture something very real and vital from the military world—but something got lost in translation. One thing for sure, Mike had no idea what hill his company was going to take. He flipped open his portfolio and below the *MENTAL* factors he had collected this morning, he wrote the words *MISSION (THE MILITARY TYPE)*.

protein for business

hey moved to one end of the weight room to work on their calf muscles. "OK," Mike began, "so I think you're on to something with this mission idea. My team and I need to do some thinking about what hill we are going to take. What else do you think causes people to bounce?" By this time Joe was drenched, and he sat down on the toe-press machine and began to mop the sweat off his head, neck, and shoulders. He sat thinking for several seconds, staring out at nothing.

"I don't know," said Joe, "come to think of it, working out in the weight room is kind of like a physical bounce, isn't it?"

"I don't follow you," said Mike.

"Think about it," Joe said, getting up a head of steam. "When you work out hard with weights, your muscles get these little tears in them—they are actually disintegrating. Your muscles get bigger and you get stronger because they are first torn down—tiny, microscopic tears. It's a physical process of disintegration and reintegration. It's the same way with people and groups. Your muscles get *weaker* before they get *stronger*. Wow, that's pretty cool," he said, obviously proud of himself.

Joe stood up and stacked an ungodly amount of weight onto the calf machine and did ten quick reps, making his peculiar *shish* sound with every extension. Mike pulled about half of the weight off the machine and sat down to do his set.

By now, Joe was on a roll. "So maybe if we think about muscle building as a metaphor for the bounce, we can figure out what else causes it. Let's start with mental toughness. Some guys come in here, and they just aren't willing to go through the pain of doing that one more set. They lack mental toughness. They don't realize that all of their strength gains come from that one extra set! Yeah, this is working. OK, now let's think about mission. What is the mission in the weight room?"

"If you don't mind, Einstein, I am going to do a quick set here while you ponder the structure of the universe," said Mike as he slipped his knees under the bar and started doing toe presses.

"I've got it!" said Joe before Mike finished his set. "How many times have you been in the weight room in the past sixty days?"

"I don't know. I've had a terrible travel schedule. Probably no more than eight or nine times," answered Mike.

"So, you're not sure how many days you've lifted, but you think it has been eight or nine, right?" asked Joe.

"Right," said Mike.

"I know *exactly* how many days I have lifted weights in the last sixty days," Joe said, talking faster. "*Exactly*. Fifty-eight. I missed a day because I had to drive my brother up to New Hampshire, and I missed a day because of Jenny's birthday. The point is, lifting weights for me is *mission* critical. If I get redeployed to Afghanistan, I had better be in shape—otherwise, someone, maybe me, will get killed. See, weight lifting is related to my mission. For you, it's a sideline. You've been doing what you should be doing—traveling all over the U.S. trying to turn your company around."

"OK, so you've proven that mental toughness and mission can be related to getting a 'muscle bounce' in the weight room. So what!" said Mike.

"So what?" asked Joe. "I'll tell you so what. I've just figured out there's a missing element in your idea of what causes the bounce," he said, poking his stubby finger into Mike's chest.

"Think about it, Mike. I've been going to weight rooms for years, and I've seen plenty of guys who have both mental toughness and mission—you know, cops, firemen, those kinds of guys. Some of them just don't seem to grow. They don't get stronger, no matter how hard they work out. And what do you think they are missing?" Joe was shouting now.

"I haven't a clue," said Mike worrying that his friend might be going off the deep end on this thing.

"Protein!" shouted Joe. "They didn't eat enough protein. The body needs protein to build up and grow the muscles!"

"So what are you saying, Joe, that we need to start every day at the office with a protein shake?"

"I'm not talking about protein *literally*," Joe said impatiently, "I'm saying you've got to figure out what the protein for *business* is. Mental toughness, mission—these are things that go on in the mind. But you can have all the mental toughness and mission in the world and it won't matter. If you aren't getting enough protein, you're just not going to grow!"

Mike started chuckling. "I think you need to lie down, Joe, get some blood flowing to your head."

saving corporate from itself

friday morning, Mike was eager to get going with the meeting, but first he knew he would have to make a difficult phone call. At 6:45, he placed a call to his boss, Rachel.

"Good morning." Rachel answered in a clipped tone, obviously busy.

"Good morning," responded Mike. "What do you have planned for the weekend?"

"In the office on Saturday getting ready for the board meeting," she responded, "and will try to spend some time with the kids on Sunday."

"Listen, Rachel, I'm calling to say that I need a little more time to get you our expense reductions."

The line went dead silent. "Mike, you have *got* to be kidding me! Do you have any idea the interference I had to run for you to get you the week extension you asked for? I'm telling you right now, this is totally unacceptable. I don't know when you decided that the rules don't apply to you, but every one of the other subsidiaries got their numbers to us a week ago, and I have been covering for you. I can't cover for you any longer."

Mike listened intently to Rachel's tirade, not at all sure what to do. Then it hit him: Absorb anxiety. *Wow,* he thought, *I not only need to be absorbing the anxiety of my own troops; there's lots of anxiety above me on the chain of command.* "I can only imagine the pressure you must be under," he said quietly.

"You have no idea," she said, her voice softening a bit. "The board is on my case big-time, and I've got investors screaming at me at every turn."

"Don't think we don't appreciate what you are doing at corporate," Mike said, shifting into heavy anxiety-absorption mode. "I'm sure the stress is several times as high as we are facing down here at the subsidiary level. And I want to say this right up front: There is no way our division is going to let you down in any way. We are determined to be one of the leaders in figuring out not just how to survive this downturn, but also to bounce back stronger than ever."

"That's what surprised me so much about your requests for these extensions, Mike; it's just not like you. You guys have always been the one group I could count on. You need to level with me on what's going on down there."

"Sending you a ten-percent expense cut today would be the easiest thing in the world to do," Mike answered. "You know that, because we have always been the first to pony up in the past. What we are trying to do right now is a whole lot harder. We are trying to bring our expenses down and at the same time position ourselves to be back in a growth mode as soon as possible. Don't worry, it isn't a matter of not making the cuts—our expenses *will* be in line. It's a matter of making the right cuts in the right ways so that the business actually comes out stronger."

"How much time do you need?"

Mike was stunned. "Just a few more days."

"Well, my presentation to the board is at nine A.M. next Friday. Finance will scream, but I guess if you got your numbers to them by nine A.M. on Thursday, they could integrate them in the presentation in the twenty-four hours we'd have left. But, Mike, understand—your numbers have to be perfect. If there is a glitch on this, there will be hell to pay."

"I understand." Mike said, hanging up the phone.

leave it to einstein

t he conference room was buzzing when Mike walked in a few minutes later for the planned all-day meeting. Someone had written a quote above Mike's diagram of the bounce on the whiteboard:

> THE SIGNIFICANT PROBLEMS WE ARE FACING CANNOT BE
> SOLVED AT THE SAME LEVEL OF THINKING WE WERE AT
> WHEN WE CREATED THEM.   —ALBERT EINSTEIN

"Cool quote!" exclaimed Mike, sitting down. "So we've all had a night to sleep on the situation here, and what are you thinking?"

Paula was the first to speak, clicking on a document on her laptop in front of her, her reading glasses pushed down on her nose. "I was up half the night running and rerunning these numbers, and, folks, the news isn't good. If we cut the ten percent out that corporate wants, plus another five percent for Altech, we are cutting not just muscle but bone."

"Don't they realize what the most recent round of cuts did to us?" asked Sean, "I can't believe they are asking for another ten percent."

"The thing that frustrates me," said Bob Fraley, chiming in, "is how far these kinds of cuts always set us back with our customers. Cuts in production equal product-quality issues. Cuts in customer service reduce our responsiveness. Cuts in product development rob us of future important innovations, which have always been our competitive edge. Sometimes I think we should just give them exactly what they are asking for at corporate. If that's what they want, let's just give it to them."

Ah, Anxiety 1 is back in the room with a vengeance, thought Mike. "So what would that look like," asked Mike, looking at Bob.

"What?" replied Bob, nervously.

"Let's go down the road you are suggesting a little bit," continued Mike. "What would it look like if we just did what corporate is asking of us?"

"We'd just keep cutting operations and customer service and product development until there was nothing left of this company but a steaming junk heap."

"Not the most compelling argument I've heard for a

point of view," said Mike, smiling. Everyone laughed, and the tension in the room eased a bit.

"You know what we are doing here," said Sean standing nervously and walking toward the whiteboard. "We are violating our own rules for creating bounce."

"How so?" asked Paula. Sean pointed to the third bullet point—*'WE CONTROL' NOT 'THEY CONTROL.'*

"We are focusing all our attention on what corporate is doing to us. The fact is, corporate didn't do anything to us. Most of us on the team have been here for five years or more. If there are problems in this company, we probably created them, and we need to be honest about that."

"So you are the source of the mysterious quote on the board," said Mike, smiling. Sean blushed and nodded.

"Speak for yourself, Sean," said Bob. "I have fought tooth and nail against every cost reduction that has been forced on us."

"With all due respect, Bob, I think Sean is on to something here," said Bill. "We all get the financial ratios from the industry trade group every year, and for the past three years, our ratios have slid compared to our competitors'. Now, how do we blame *that* on corporate? We're the ones running the business, and if we can't run our business at least as well as our competitors— and hopefully a whole lot better—then corporate should probably replace us and bring in some people from those competitors who can." The room went silent. "Every year we have told ourselves *and* have told corporate that we are going to grow our way into better ratios. There's always some new product or some new market that is going to save the day. The same story year after year. When are we going to get real with ourselves here? We are not going to grow our way into better performance. We need to fix the business and then grow on that healthy platform."

Sean was still awkwardly standing at the whiteboard, and no one really knew why, but suddenly he jumped to life. "Hey, that's number one under *MENTAL!*" He pointed to the board. "See things as they really are!" Everyone began to nod.

"No matter which way you slice it," said Paula, a little sadly, "it all comes back to money. Money is the fuel that businesses run on. Until we fix our money problems, we are not going to make much progress."

"That's it!" shouted Mike, jumping to his feet, "It's money! Money is *protein* for business." The room looked at him as if he had just ripped off all his clothes.

"Protein?" asked Bill, "What are you talking about?" Mike rushed to the board, nearly knocking down Sean, who was still inexplicably standing in front of it. He picked up a different colored marker and added the word.

REINTEGRATION

DISINTEGRATION

MENTAL

- SEE REALITY CLEARLY.
- TREAT CAUSES, NOT SYMPTOMS (DON'T JUST DO SOMETHING: STAND THERE).
- "WE CONTROL," NOT "THEY CONTROL."
- HOLD HANDS IN TRAFFIC.

MONEY

"OK, forget the whole protein thing," Mike said excitedly, deciding it would be just too hard to retrace the winding route Joe had taken him on in the weight room the night before. "We've been focused on what corporate is taking from us—the overhead charge, the cost cuts, the centralization of key services. Instead we should be focused on how our business *creates* money, and how it is going to create money in the future."

"Paula's right!" he continued. "Money *is* the fuel that all business runs on, and we haven't been focused enough on how to put more fuel in our tank. And Bill's right too. We're so busy worrying about the fuel others are taking

away from us—competitors taking money by stealing our
clients, customers taking our fuel when they push for
price concessions, corporate taking our money. . . . Folks,
we haven't been running this business strategically. If
we had been, we'd be reporting ratios that would put our
competitors to shame."

"That makes a lot of sense," Paula said cautiously, "but
I'm not sure we have the luxury of thinking in those terms
right now. We have reality to deal with here. You should
hear the things that corporate finance is saying about us
right now. We are the only subsidiary that hasn't delivered
our expense cuts. They're saying that you are just refusing to
cut—and, Mike, that makes me really nervous."

"I haven't refused anything, Paula. Our division has
always led this company in terms of doing our part, of
being good corporate citizens, and we are not going to
stop now. But we are not going to build our lives around
hitting deadlines at the expense of doing what's right for
this company. Too many people are depending on us. Now
let's get to work generating a list of options on how we
can size this business to the revenue levels we are likely to
see next year and how to do it in a way that improves our
competitive position."

"That's all?" asked Bob. "Then we should be done by
lunch." Everyone laughed. Paula began handing out budget

reports, Bob distributed the sales forecasts, and they all settled in for a long day.

Mike had pizzas delivered for lunch, and except for an occasional bathroom break, no one left the room, not even for a moment. By about six P.M., the walls of the conference room were covered with flip-chart paper, and people were looking bedraggled. The mood in the room began to darken.

"Folks," Mike finally said, "if this were easy, everyone would be a senior executive. This is why we make the big bucks. I think we should all head home, spend the weekend with our families, and start fresh on Monday. Anyone who can't clear their calendars on Monday? Bob, are we going to mess up your tee time?" They all managed a tired chuckle as they filed out of the room.

As the room emptied, Mike copied down key points from the flip-chart pages that covered all four walls of the conference room. He stared at his pad. They were no closer to solving the problem than they had been when they started in the morning.

my life as a tool

even though they seemed to have made little progress, Mike was upbeat when he walked in the front door of his home that evening. He heard the voices of his wife, Mary, and his oldest daughter, Gracie, echoing from the kitchen. "I told you on Monday—no sleepover this weekend if you didn't finish your report!" Mary shouted. "What part of that conversation did you miss?"

"Quit trying to control me," screamed Gracie. "You're such a control freak! The report isn't due till Tuesday!"

"Hey, guys," Mike said quietly, picking up a celery stick from the kitchen table and crunching it loudly. Gracie was standing at the counter, her skinny gazelle legs sticking out from beneath her plaid private-school uniform.

"Will you please tell your daughter that she is not going to Chelsea's tomorrow night unless she finishes her report?" Mary said loudly.

"You heard the woman, princess. Best get cracking," Mike said cheerfully.

"Get cracking? Who *says* that? What are you, from the nineteenth century? Dad, you're such a *tool!*"

Mike felt his anger flash, and then he saw it: *anxiety.*

"That's right, I'm a *tool.* And you better hope I'm a *hammer,*" he said, pounding playfully on the top of her head, "and not a *wrench*"—he grabbed her in a headlock and twisted her head from side to side. He sat down beside her.

"Sooooo lame, Dad," Gracie said rolling her eyes. Mike was struck by just how dramatically two eyes could roll.

He crunched another celery stick absentmindedly. "So tell me what's bothering you, princess," Mike said, smiling.

"What's bothering me is that you guys can't stop controlling me. I'm thirteen years old and you treat me like I'm seven! I'm sick of it—I wish you and Mom would just get a life!" Mike sat back in his chair and stared at Gracie, then looked quickly to Mary and winked.

"I *saw* that," spat Gracie.

"So maybe you're right," Mike said finally. "Maybe its time you started getting a bit more control of your life. Would you like that?"

Gracie rolled her eyes again. "Duh."

"Yep, we need to start treating you like the adult you are becoming." Mary shot him a nervous glance that said *Where are you going with this, genius?*

"So here's how the adult world works. Every day I go to

work, I make a choice on how hard to work. And the choice I make determines what kind of life I'm going to have. If I want an A life—one that allows me to live in this big house, drive nice cars, and send my girls to fancy private schools—I have to achieve an A performance in work. If I am happy with a B life, I can get away with B performance, but I'm going to end up living in a different neighborhood, sending you girls to public schools—well, you get the picture."

"And a C life?" Gracie asked.

"Well, it wouldn't be something out of Charles Dickens, but you and your sister would definitely have way different wardrobe options," he said, his eyes twinkling.

Gracie punched his arm and smiled. "Well, let's go, Dad! Shoot for an A-plus life! You know I've got my eye on an Ebel watch." It was Mom's turn to roll her eyes.

"So, Mary," Mike said, looking at his wife, "I think it's time we put Gracie here on the adult program." Gracie had been listening with one ear, the other being plugged with an iPod earbud pumping out hip-hop that Mike could hear all the way across the table. She popped the earbud out and turned toward him.

Time to convert Anxiety 1 to Anxiety 2, thought Mike. "Here's how it will work, Grace. You get to pick the kind of life you want by the kind of effort you want to put out. A effort equals an A life—which includes sleepovers, unlimited phone time, use of one of the cell phones, having your friends over—a pretty cool life. B effort gets you a B life—still very livable, but not quite as sweet as the A program."

"And a C life?" Gracie asked nervously. Mike smiled.

"Well, the good news is, you'll get to spend a lot of quality time with your family."

"Well, given *that* option, you know I'll be getting good grades," Gracie retorted sarcastically. "So you're saying you would really let me get Cs?"

"If that's the life you choose," said Mike. Mary winced.

"But, Dad," Gracie said, "if I get Cs, I won't be able to get into a good college. I won't ever see my friends!" *Great, Anxiety 2 on the rise,* thought Mike.

"I understand that, Gracie, and your mom and I would be really sad if that was the choice you made. But when a person gets to be your age, they have to start making their own decisions and start living with the consequences."

Gracie looked out the window to the backyard and watched the dog running around with a tennis ball. A look of anxiety crossed her face. "Dad, what if I get in a really tough class, like trigonometry or something, and I just don't understand it?"

"Then we'll get you a tutor. All we ask is that you give it your best—it's our job to make sure you have all the resources you need to do it."

"It still seems kind of lame to me," she said, popping her earbud back in and standing up to leave the room.

"Hey, I just got home. Where you going?"

"To work on my re*port*."

Mary moved around behind Mike, put her arms around his neck, and kissed the top of his head. "What did you just do?" she asked.

"I just converted Anxiety 1 to Anxiety 2," he answered.

"Come again?"

Mike kissed her hand. "Secret military stuff. You wouldn't understand it."

She hugged him tighter. "Well if you keep doing things like that, I may dump this other guy I'm seeing."

Mike leaned back to look into her eyes and grinned. "There's only one?"

vexed in the city

The family spent a relaxed Saturday morning together. Gracie finished up her book report while Mary and their other daughter made breakfast and cleaned the kitchen. Mary found Mike in the garage, tinkering with his Harley.

"TV's on the fritz again," she said, drying her hands with a dish towel. "I think we should go ahead and get that flat-screen we've been talking about."

Mike looked up and began wiping grease from his hands. "Just in time for the Super Bowl! Great idea."

Mike wasn't normally much of a shopper, but a trip to Digital City was different. He could get lost for hours there, browsing the aisles looking at cool electronic equipment, sleek new laptops, and computer and iPod accessories. Around eleven A.M., he jumped into Mary's SUV and headed for the Digital City just off Route 124.

The parking lot was packed. *Forgot that Saturday is geek day,* Mike thought. Entering the brightly lit store, he turned right to face the twenty-five-foot-high floor-to-ceiling display of flat-screen TVs. There must have been nearly a hundred models, all tuned to the same channel, creating a dizzying effect of synchronized splashing colors. Mike began walking along the wall, comparing picture quality and prices. He paused in front of his dream set, a sixty-inch Sony LCD. *Wish I had measured the space on the den wall,* he thought. *Not sure we have room for the sixty.*

"Sony's way overpriced," a voice behind him said. "Samsung's the best brand for your money right now." Assuming the voice was speaking to someone else, Mike continued to read the specification card next to the set. "But hey, Bro, if you've got money to burn, the Japanese economy could use a boost right now."

Bro? Mike spun around to see Joe standing there grinning, wearing a ridiculous bright red Digital City uniform shirt and a name tag that read GI JOE.

"Joe?" Mike stammered, "What . . . what are you doing here?"

"I work here," Joe responded. "This is my stateside gig."

"Why?" Mike asked, immediately regretting the question.

"Not much demand for professional killers here in the Boston area," Joe said, laughing, "except for over on the South Side."

"What's with the name tag?" Mike tried changing the subject.

"Shift manager likes bustin' my chops. So you looking for a TV?"

Mike struggled to regain his composure. "Ah, yeah . . . we've been . . . thought it was time to step up to a flat screen."

Joe was unfazed. "Well, we've got some killer deals right now, if you like to finance stuff—no payments for almost a year."

Mike was feeling more and more awkward with each passing moment. "Hey, Joe, I'm sorry for . . . well, for being so surprised . . . you know, when you run into someone in a place you are not used to seeing them . . . kind of takes a moment to connect."

"No problem, Bro. At your age, Alzheimer's is starting to kick in. What can I show you?"

"What I meant to say is that I'm sorry for being surprised that you're working here. You're just so incredibly *capable*. I mean, you've given me some of the best advice of my life."

"You're not one of those guys who think all the capable people are in the fancy corner offices, are you, Mike?"

"No, . . . of course not," he stammered, feeling even more embarrassed. *Just shut up,* he told himself.

"Good," said Joe, flashing a good-natured smile, "'cause if you get to know them, some of the guys on the floor here have capabilities that would blow you away. See that guy in the ponytail over there in Computers? That's Raul. There is nothing that guy can't take apart and put back together. That little guy over there with the glasses? Dude's name is Roger. Guy was a rock star in the hacker community by the time he was fifteen—goes by the screen name Zoltan."

Mike finally listened to the voice in his head and kept his mouth shut.

"Now, let's get you into a TV," Joe said. "Jenny would kill me if I let a walking fat commission like you walk out the door." Joe helped Mike load a monster fifty-six-inch Samsung into Mary's SUV. (Joe advised against the sixty-inch; said it might make people think Mike was trying to compensate for something.) It wouldn't fit in the back, so Joe showed Mike how to pop off the headrests, and they slid the set over the top of both sets of backseats.

For the rest of the weekend, Mike couldn't get his encounter with Joe at Digital City out of his mind. He was still embarrassed at what he had said to Joe as he recovered from the shock of bumping into him there. Mike worried that he might have insulted him. More than anything, he felt like a bad friend. Joe knew so much about Mike and CRX, and it wasn't until this morning that Mike realized he hadn't even asked Joe what he did for a living.

the last twenty people on the boat

S itting in his office early Monday morning, Mike was still thinking about the weekend encounter. He was over the guilt, but he was struck by what Joe had said. *If you get to know them, some of the guys on the floor here have capabilities that would blow you away.* Mike got up from his desk and walked out of his office. He went down the back stairwell and walked across the alley and into the side door of the production facility. The huge, warehouse-size space was buzzing with activity. The night shift would be going strong for about the next half hour. He walked along the production lines, and as people on the line looked up, he nodded and smiled. As he met each face, he found himself wondering, *Is there another Joe behind that face? What special capabilities does this person have that the rest of us are totally unaware of?* The night-shift crew weren't used to seeing Mike on the line, and after a few minutes, José, one of the line managers, walked up to him.

"Everything OK, Mike?" José asked.

"Everything's great, José. Just here to see how the folks

who actually *make* our stuff are doing." José smiled proudly. Several of the line supervisors walked up and joined them, and Mike chatted with them easily, asking questions about the orders that had been run that night. He looked at his watch.

"Wow, 7:35, gotta go, guys. I'm late to my own meeting!" Walking back up the stairs, he suddenly knew what he was going to do.

The executive team was waiting for him when he walked into the conference room. "Anybody wake up in the middle of the night this weekend with the magic solution?" Mike asked on the way to his chair. The room went silent. "Me neither," he said. "So we are going to bring in some more brains."

"Consultants?" asked Bill, wrinkling his nose.

Mike turned and faced the group smiling. "I said we are going to bring in more *brains*, not *pains*." Everyone laughed.

"Here's what we are going to do," explained Mike. "We have some very capable people in this company who aren't in this room right now. We're going to get them in the room, and we're going to get them to help us think this through. We're going to make a list right now of the people we think are the smartest, most committed, and most creative people in our company. And we are going to spend the morning getting people to cover for them in their jobs so that they can join us here at one P.M."

"But, Mike," Bill protested, "most of the people below our level really don't understand the strategic issues."

"So we'll spend a couple of hours bringing them up to speed. What they do know, Bill, is our business. Each of them knows something about our customers, our technologies, our products, or our markets that might be helpful."

"Mike, have you really thought this through?" asked Paula, shifting nervously in her seat. "I mean, we really can't talk about strategic options without revealing the reality of our situation—and the fact that there will probably be layoffs."

"Good point, Paula," said Mike, looking right at her, "so we need to make sure we have absolute trust that they will respect the confidentiality of the situation."

"But, Mike," Paula continued, "what if one of the people in the room ends up being one of the people whose job we decide to eliminate?"

"Another good point," said Mike, "so let's say the people we invite to join us should be the twenty people we think should be the last twenty people on this boat before it goes down. The twenty most indispensable people in the company."

"Can we make it twenty-one and throw Bob off the boat now?" asked Paula.

"Not without my swim trunks," said Bob.

As they began to create the list, it was slow going, but

after a few minutes, the group began to pick up the pace. Within about a half hour, the executives had fanned out across the building to notify people in their department that they were needed for the afternoon.

too many hills

just before one P.M., Mike walked down the hall
toward the meeting room and noticed the huge
teak conference-room table lying on its side in the hall. *The
thing must weigh fifteen hundred pounds,* he thought. *How
in the world did they get it out into the hall?* There was a
jumble of chairs pushed to the center of the room, but the
people inside were all on their feet. The room was buzzing
when he walked in, packed with small groups talking and
gesturing around flip-chart pages. The room fell silent as
Mike entered.

He looked around the room. An eclectic collection of
salespeople, operations supervisors, product managers,
accounting people—all of them familiar faces. The executive
team had done a good job of picking the best and the
brightest on short notice.

"Thank you all for rearranging your day," Mike said
quietly, walking toward the whiteboard. "I'd like to ask
all of you a question. Think of a personal quality that you
as an individual have that you are most proud of," he said,

looking around the room. "Now I know that most of us have a hard time talking about our qualities. It's supposed to be immodest—and I'm not going to call on anyone—but I'd like to know if there is anyone in the room who is willing to share what personal quality they thought of." Silence. Mike began to get nervous. *What if nobody volunteers?*

Finally, in the back of the room, Trisha from accounting raised her hand tentatively. She blushed when everyone looked her way. "Well," she said, "my friends say I am really loyal."

"Loyalty," said Mike, relieved that someone had spoken up. "Now, Trish, I want to ask you a second, even harder question. How do you think it is that you became so loyal?"

Trisha looked startled. "Gee, I don't know, that really *is* a hard question."

"Two extra vacation days this quarter if you answer it," Mike responded.

"In *that* case," she squealed and everyone laughed. After a few moments, she said, "Well, . . . it's kind of personal. . . . When I was ten, my mom and dad split up, and it was really hard for me . . . but something inside of me was determined to have a good relationship with both my mom and my dad. So I really focused on being loyal to both of them, and I learned, maybe younger than most, that when you are loyal to someone, you can usually make things work."

"Thanks so much for sharing that with us, Trish. There

is now a roomful of people here who will resent you all quarter for those two extra vacation days." More laughter. "You've just illustrated something we as an executive team have been talking about the past week or so. The fact is, often it is when times are toughest that we develop some of our most important capabilities. We think it is true for people and it is true for companies. Now, I don't need to tell you all that our company is going through a very tough time here, but the team and I are convinced that if we handle this current challenge right, we are going to not only survive it, we are going to discover capabilities that we didn't even know we have."

Mike uncapped a marker and pointed to the board. "We've been talking for the past few days about what allows some companies to bounce back quickly from hardships while others don't. And we're trying to identify the things that give great companies their bounce," he said, tracing the shape of the bounce and explaining the concepts of disintegration and reintegration.

"We think one of the most important factors is the ability to see things clearly, to not be in a state of denial." He gestured toward *MENTAL* written on the whiteboard. "If there is a problem, we want to face it head-on. We never want to run from the truth, no matter how hard it might be to hear." Mike quickly described the other aspects of mental toughness that determine a company's bounce.

"The second factor we talked about is money. Now I know some people think it is not polite to talk about money, but the fact of the matter is that great companies generate a lot of money that can be poured back into new products, new services, and other types of growth. Not-so-great companies aren't as good at generating money, and over the long term, they lose the race and go out of business. Now I want to stop right there and ask if there is anyone who will be uncomfortable if we have a brutally honest conversation about this company's declining performance in generating money for our growth."

A deep and heavily accented voice rose from the back of the room. It was Big Tony, a line lead for the day shift. Tony is a six-foot-six-inch Hispanic who grew up on the rough streets of Los Angeles and weighs over three hundred pounds, so it goes without saying that when Tony speaks, people listen. "We've been talking too *little* about money these days—*that's* the problem."

"What do you mean, Tony?" asked Mike, bending sideways see Tony's face through the crowd.

"We all see the numbers that compare us to the other companies, and we know we're slipping. So I'm actually kind of *relieved* we're talking about this stuff."

"Great," said Mike, thinking, *Big Tony is definitely one of our Joes.*

"I want to add one more 'M' to the white board." Mike

wrote the words *MISSION (THE MILITARY TYPE)* and stood back and looked at the board for a moment.

REINTEGRATION

DISINTEGRATION

MENTAL

· *SEE REALITY CLEARLY.*
· *TREAT CAUSES, NOT SYMPTOMS (DON'T JUST DO SOMETHING; STAND THERE).*
· *"WE CONTROL," NOT "THEY CONTROL."*
· *HOLD HANDS IN TRAFFIC.*

MONEY

MISSION (THE MILITARY TYPE)

"In order for us to be successful here, we need to determine our mission. Now I'm not talking about our mission statement or some list of platitudes. An army platoon might be given a mission to take a certain hill by a certain deadline. The question I am asking is, as a team, what hill are we going to take, and how are we going to take it?"

Tony spoke up again. "That's the whole problem! We've

been trying to take *all* the hills. We need to decide which hill is most important."

Mike smiled at Tony and then looked around the room. "Well, that's exactly the kind of thing we have brought you all in here to help us figure out."

going to war

ike looked at his watch. *Good, I only talked for five minutes.* He sat down and began to roll up his shirtsleeves. "On the walls around you are all the scenarios we as an executive team could think of. We don't think any of these scenarios are good enough. We don't feel that we have complete clarity on the issues. We are going to move around the room together, stopping at each scenario, and each of the vice presidents is going to take a turn at one of the scenarios—running through the numbers with you, giving you the assumptions. We won't move on until we are sure that everyone in the room understands the scenario. You *cannot* be shy about this. If you don't understand something, you *must* tell us. We will not be able to take our thinking to a new level with your new ideas until we all understand the issues."

The process took hours. With each scenario, there was a myriad of questions. It was obvious that many people in operations did not have a clue what the company's sales strategies were, and vice versa. Mike made a note on his pad:

How do we make sure in the future that everyone understands how the pieces of the business fit together?—something he would think about later.

As the afternoon wore on, Mike began to notice something. The questions were getting better. The people in the room were getting their heads around the business in just a matter of hours. His mind had drifted a bit during the presentation of the first couple of scenarios, but by the fourth, his attention was riveted to the discussion. But just as the group began to pick up momentum, Mike looked at his watch and saw that it was almost five P.M. He interrupted the discussion.

"Folks, I just noticed that it is five o'clock, and I realize that many of you in the room probably have child-care commitments and what have you, so we are going to need to find a time when we can pick this back up."

One of the salesmen swiveled his chair around and said, "Mike, I think it would be a mistake to cut this off right now. I mean, we are just starting to get somewhere." A chorus of voices rose in support.

"OK, let's do this: Anyone who wants to stay tonight and work this through is welcome to stay. Anyone who can't stay because of other commitments, we totally understand, and we will make sure we bring you up to date on any progress we make when you come in tomorrow." Mike looked at the members of the executive team and asked, "You OK with that?" They all nodded eagerly. Mike called a thirty-minute break so people could call home and make any arrangements they might need to make in order to work through the evening, and he asked Susan to order a delivery of Chinese food from the restaurant down the street.

At five-thirty, the group reconvened, and Mike realized after a few minutes that *everyone* had stayed. By seven, Sean Tinsley was finishing the last scenario. A small table had been dragged into a corner of the room, where it sat overflowing with empty food containers and soda cans. Mike felt the fatigue kicking in and with it a mild sense of hopelessness. Had this whole thing been a mistake? What did he hope to gain by having a bunch of lower-level people sit through an explanation of scenarios his senior executives had hashed out just days before. *People might leave this room feeling worse than when they came in,* he worried. *This could be a royal bust.*

Sean was winding down. "So, with this scenario, like the others, we are still going to cut expenses by fifteen percent— ten percent as required by the new corporate mandate and five percent for the loss of the Altech account."

Mike's impatience flared, and he interrupted. "Sean, we are not cutting expenses due to a corporate mandate. We are cutting expenses because our business isn't performing at the level that it was two years ago. If it was, there would be

no corporate mandate. We can't blame corporate for this."
The room was silent.

"I want to talk about that other number," said Trish from
accounting, pushing her glasses farther up on her nose. "I
have run the numbers—do you realize that we were not
making any money on the Altech account?"

"That doesn't make any sense, Trish," Mike said. "The
gross margins for Altech are about average."

"You're right, Mike. The *gross* margins are fine, but if
you look at the indirect costs, it's a different story. Jack and
I did a study a couple of weeks ago. When you factor in the
time people in customer support and product management
were spending on that account, I calculate that we actually
lost money—roughly ten cents for every dollar of revenue."
She walked over to Mike and handed him a page with an
Excel spreadsheet on it.

"Have you seen these numbers, Paula?" Mike asked.

"Trish was just going over them with me this morning,"
said Paula. "She is right on this one." Mike sat back stunned.

"It's not just Altech," said Sally. "When I saw Trish's
report, I realized that we haven't been doing a very good
job accounting for indirect costs. There's a whole class of
customers just like Altech."

"I can tell you exactly who those companies are," said
Jack, the new manager of the customer-support group, as he
flipped open his laptop. "When Trish asked me to team up

with her on the study, we created a list of companies that consume huge amounts of our customer-support resources. We figured out that sixty percent of our staff's time is taken up by only twenty of our clients."

"Altech isn't the worst," added Trish. "We have three clients that, if you account for all the costs correctly, are costing up to fifteen cents for every dollar of revenue."

"I gotta see those numbers," shouted Sales Chief Bob Fraley from the other side of the room. Trisha walked a copy over to him, and he pulled on his reading glasses and studied the sheet intently. After a couple of minutes, he said, "This changes everything. We need to get people on planes *tomorrow* to visit these customers and get some price concessions. Most of these companies are good companies— they don't want their vendors to go out of business. I believe they will work with us."

"The question is, do *we* want to work with *them*?" It was Bart, one of the product-development engineers. Until this very moment, nobody could remember him saying a word all day.

"What do you mean?" Bill asked.

"Trish showed me a copy of the report when she and Jack finished their study," Bart continued. "She wanted to know if the same companies gobbled up lots of product-development time too. They didn't, but I noticed they had one thing in common: They are all buying simple assemblies of commodity products from us. I'm not sure that's a game we want to play. We used to be innovators—that's where I think we really shine."

"I totally agree with Bart on this," said Leslie, a young dynamo of a saleswoman sitting in the front row. "I joined this company because it was a leader in technology. I have a client right now that is spending a million dollars a year with us. They want to spend ten million a year with us, but they need us to integrate some proprietary technology into our systems for them—and we can't get it through the product-development queue."

"Well, now we know why," exclaimed Mike—"because we're operating a nonprofit division for twenty of our customers!"

"There are lots of customers like Leslie's. People looking for value-added solutions," said Sean. "We should build our business around *those* kinds of customers!"

The facts were clicking into place in Mike's brain like tumblers on the lock of a safe. A powerful new strategy, a *mission* for the company, was appearing out of thin air. *Instant reintegration.* He hadn't expected reintegration to happen this way, all at once, in a blinding flash of insight. His mind struggled to keep track of the jumble of numbers and ideas and angles. He glanced up at the clock: Ten thirty. *No wonder I feel so tired.*

Suddenly Bill jumped to his feet. "We've got our *mission*

right here, folks. Here it is, clear as day," he said, pointing to Trish's report. The room murmured in agreement.

"I'm going to want some time to plug in some new numbers," Paula said, clicking open her laptop.

"I've got an idea," said Sally. "Mike, give us till Wednesday noon, and we'll nail the mission and the money issues." *Wednesday noon.* Mike's mind struggled through the fog of fatigue. *But I've got to give Rachel the numbers by Thursday morning. If there's anything wrong in what they come up with, we won't have time to fix it.*

"How about it, Mike?" asked Bob Fraley. "Are you going to trust us or not?"

"Yes, Bob," replied Mike wearily. "That's exactly what I *am* going to do. I'm going to trust you."

"Before we go, Mike, can I say one thing?" It was Big Tony from production.

"Sure, Tony. What is it?"

"I just want to thank you for what you did for us—all of us here today. When you do stuff like this—let us all help figure things out—well, it's really been incredible. I just want you to know that I have always loved this company, but tonight, I'd go to *war* for this company." *Go to war,* Mike thought. *Interesting choice of words.* The group broke into spontaneous applause, and Mike sat silently, his emotions welling up inside of him.

an unbroken tiebreaker

throughout the next day, the office was a flurry of activity. The conference-room table stayed propped awkwardly on its side near the conference-room entrance. People had to turn sideways to get past it in the hall. One group after another jockeyed for time in the conference room and in the training room, but demand was too great. Ad hoc meetings sprang up around the atrium, flip-chart paper covering every available wall.

Every time Mike walked by a meeting, the temptation to take a seat and jump in on the conversation was overwhelming, but he kept his distance. He said he was going to trust his team members, and that's what he was going to do.

He met Joe for a workout in the weight room early that night. The sting of his faux pas at Digital City was gone, and between sets he eagerly regaled Joe with all that had happened the day before. He told him how he had called together the group of middle managers and frontline people, how they had struggled for hours reviewing one

seemingly hopeless scenario after another, and how surprised
he had been to learn that some of the frontline people
had been stressing for more than a year that the company
wasn't paying enough attention to its declining financial
performance. Finally, he told Joe about that moment, around
ten thirty P.M., when all the pieces seemed to fall into
place—how, although they couldn't all articulate it perfectly,
everyone in the room seemed to sense that they had found
their mission. Mike talked and talked and talked, losing all
awareness of time. Every once in a while, when he would
make an important point, Joe would look up and smile and
say, "Hooah, Bro."

"And you are not going to believe how the meeting
ended," said Mike, beginning to wind down. "This big guy
from operations—they call him Big Tony—he stands up and
thanks me. Thanks me for putting him through the sixteen-
hour ordeal. Can you believe that? And guess what he says
as he is leaving. He says, "Today, I would go to war for this
company."

Joe smiled. "How big is Big Tony? Maybe we could use
him over there."

As Mike reached into his portfolio to pull out his
weight-training card, Joe noticed the notes on Mike's pad.
"Hey, let me see that," Joe said, snatching the pad from
Mike's hands. He stared at it thoughtfully.

"You know, Mike, you are still missing an M."

"I am?" said Mike.

"Yeah, mental toughness, money—the protein of business—I knew you'd use my idea! And mission—but you're still missing one."

"What am I missing?" asked Mike.

"Probably the most important M of all, Mike. I thought of it when you told me about Big Tony. When someone tells you they'd go to war for something, they are telling you about their morale. But be careful with that word Mike, because just like the word *mission, morale* is a military word. And geniuses in the business world tend to screw up the translation of *morale* as badly as they do the word *mission*."

"How so?" asked Mike.

"The bonehead brass at Digital City are always talking about what they are going to do to improve morale. 'We're going to throw a pizza party to improve morale,' they say. They send you a card on your birthday, stuff like that. I call it moron morale, because only a moron could convince himself that this stuff had anything to do with morale." Mike burst out laughing.

"Now I'm not saying that there is anything wrong with parties or birthday cards, and I'm sure the people who dream this stuff up probably mean well. But if Digital City really understood what morale was, they'd be focused on figuring out how to stop our competitors from eating our lunch in the marketplace. That's what really frosts the guys on the sales floor—losing our best salespeople to those clowns across the street."

"So what is morale, in the military sense?" asked Mike.

"It's just like what Big Tony said—something worth fighting for," replied Joe. "Always ask yourself if you are giving people something worth fighting for. With him, you obviously did."

"So how does a leader build morale among his troops?" asked Mike.

Joe thought for a moment and looked down at Mike's pad in his hands. "Seems like you've got a great start right here," said Joe. "Mental toughness is important. When a leader sees things as they really are, I think, that's the kind of leader I want to follow—he pushes me to get to the root cause of things; he seizes the initiative himself instead of blaming outside forces, and he expects me to do the same. Hold hands in traffic . . . let's see . . . to me that might mean always putting the good of the outfit before yourself. And nothing, I mean *nothing* builds morale faster than a compelling mission that everyone understands and believes in. And, Mike, when you do what you did yesterday, when you involve people in the key decisions that affect their lives, when you respect their abilities so much that you ask for their help solving the biggest problems you are facing, people will run through walls for you." Mike grabbed the pad from Joe and scribbled the final M on the pad: *MORALE (THE MILITARY TYPE)*.

"By the way, Bro, all this talk of morale reminds me," Joe said. "I'm shipping out next week."

"Shipping out?" Mike asked, looking up from his pad, "What, is Digital City raising a militia?"

"No, I'm in the reserves, and my reserve unit is getting deployed to Afghanistan."

Mike stood in stunned silence. He realized at that moment just how much he was going to miss his friend. "I didn't even know you were in the reserves," Mike said quietly.

"It's what I do," said Joe, smiling.

As they walked by an empty racquetball court, Joe's face broke into a mischievous grin. "You know, we never settled our racquetball score."

They grabbed their racquets and stepped onto the court ready for the grudge match to end all grudge matches. Within minutes, they were both soaked with sweat and panting heavily. Joe was a bull of a man, clearly the superior specimen in the weight room or on a run, but Mike's skill on the court made them nearly dead even. This match was going to be won by a hair, and by heart. Just as in their earlier match, Joe jumped out to an early lead, but Mike battled back furiously. Their heads spun as they dove for shots and went crashing into the walls and occasionally into each other.

It was 10–10 in the tiebreaker. Joe pointed his chin to the ceiling and walked in little circles at the service line, gasping for breath. He bent over, his hands on his knees, panting, the sweat running off him onto the floor. Suddenly he stood up straight and smiled.

"Hey, you know, it was exactly at this point last time that you broke my friggin' nose." Mike was so winded he couldn't even respond. Joe crouched down to serve. Mike shuffled his feet to life. Joe stood up again.

"Or," Joe said, "we could just leave it like this."

Mike immediately recognized the beauty of the gesture. This wasn't a point in a game either man wanted to win. This was a point in time they wanted to share. Joe threw his arm over Mike's shoulder, and the two men walked off the court.

company on a mission

a s he walked toward the conference room, Mike heard people talking loudly and noticed a jumble of chairs in the hall stacked nearly four feet high next to the upended table. When he walked in, he was immediately struck by the number of people present. *There are many more people here than there were on Monday night,* he thought. They were all standing. The room went quiet as he walked in.

"We had to lose the chairs," Sean said loudly, moving to meet Mike at the door. "And we had to deputize some additional people, but don't worry, they all know this stuff is strictly confidential." *That explains all these people,* Mike thought. "Everyone in this room played an important role in what you are about to see," Sean added. He looked toward Sally, standing at the far end of the room near a small table and LCD projector. In unison, people moved to clear a patch for the image about to be projected onto the far wall.

Sally cleared her throat. "I'm told you like it short and sweet, Mike, so we are going to show you only two slides. I am going to do the money slide, and Bob is going to do the mission slide."

She hit a button on her laptop, and a slide titled "MONEY" lit up the wall.

"Corporate has been asking us for expense cuts," she began, "but what they really want is free cash flow. When we ran the numbers on what they were asking, it totaled $2.5 million in additional cash flow for the year. We are going to give them $4.0 million."

Mike wrinkled his nose. "How are we going to do that?"

Sally clicked her laptop, revealing the first line of the slide. "Remember those twenty clients that Trish identified as poor profit performers? Well, Bob and his team have talked to *all* of them. Based on his analysis, we believe that thirteen of them are going to agree to price concessions. More important, they are firms our company should really be working with in the future. Bob believes we can gravitate toward the kind of high-technology, integrated products and services that Leslie's customer is demanding."

"What about the other seven customers?" Mike asked.

"We are going to fire them," was Sally's response. Several in the room immediately sensed Mike tensing up and began nodding in support of the idea. "We're going to be nice about it," Sally quickly added. "We are going to help them transition to another vendor—over whatever time-frame they need."

"Well, getting some price concessions from a few customers isn't going to add up to $4 million and losing the revenue from the other seven clients is going to put you even deeper in the hole."

"We know that," she said, clicking the button to reveal the next line on the slide.

"There are going to have to be some spending cuts. We think we need to reduce the size of the customer-support group by thirty people. We just won't need that big a staff when we get rid of these seven resource hogs."

"OK, so we are still not anywhere near $4 million."

Sally clicked the button again and turned to Big Tony. "Tony, why don't you take this next point?"

Tony moved toward the wall where the image was projected. "Mike, we quantified the savings we have produced with the Lean Manufacturing project over the last six weeks on the first shift. The first shift leads have agreed to migrate to the other shifts and locations so we can accelerate Lean across the company. By doing this, the savings will be huge."

Sally continued through her slide, Mike peppering her and the group with questions on every proposed initiative. Their thinking was rock solid. Their numbers made sense.

Sally clicked to reveal the last line, and Mike, a math whiz, quickly totaled up the numbers on the slide. "Sally," he interrupted her, "this stuff adds up to $5.5 million in additional free cash flow. What gives."

"We are going to reinvest $1.5 million of that cash in a new initiative, in the form of some equipment and seven new people for product development."

"Good luck with that," Mike said sarcastically.

"Well, to understand our thinking, we need to move to the mission slide."

Bob took his place next to the LCD projector and walked Mike through a proposed mission for the company: It called for CRX to begin moving out of commodity-based customer relationships and moving toward high-value-added integrated systems for clients. Among other things, Bob explained that as customers migrated to this new approach, the customers could do their own monitoring and managing of the systems, greatly reducing drain on customer-support and product-development resources.

"Leslie and I and the product development team had a long talk with Leslie's client who wants us to build this integrated system for them," said Bob. "They are ready to pull the trigger on a joint development contract. All we have to do is show we are serious about it." Mike pushed and probed and prodded, shooting questions at people around the room. Try as he might, he just couldn't find a weakness.

He moved to the front of the room and paced back and forth, his face taking on the shapes and colors of the slide every time he crossed in front of the projector. He stopped and looked into the sea of faces. "Guys, an *incredibly* good job. I mean it. You really stepped up." Smiles broke out around the room. He turned to Paula. "How long will it take you to package up the spreadsheets so I can go through them?"

"Already done." She stepped forward and handed him a flash drive.

"Great," he said, a little startled. "If these numbers add up, how long will it take you to get them to Corporate Finance?"

Paula blushed. "Ah, Mike, about that . . . the folks in Finance were getting really antsy, so I sent these numbers to them last night." The room exploded in laughter. "But," she shouted, "in my defense, they promised to hold them until you gave the green light."

Mike looked at Sally. "Sally, I'm feeling a little redundant here. You got a spot for me out on the line?" More laughter.

joe ships out

The next week was a whirlwind of activity. The numbers checked out, and Rachel made her presentation to the board, thrilled that Mike had found an extra $1.5 million. She had initially resisted making an exception for Mike on the hiring freeze, so Mike talked her into flying down with Bob, Leslie, and the product-development team when they met with Leslie's client, so she could hear with her own ears the kind of opportunity they would be passing up. Leslie stepped out of the meeting after only twenty minutes to send a text to the corporate finance department:

L   Approve the positions.

Mike and Joe had planned to get together before Joe shipped out, but with everything going on in the office and with all Joe had to do to prepare for the trip, it just didn't happen. But they did speak by phone briefly on the day that Joe was to leave.

Mike was really struggling with the layoffs. He had done layoffs before, but in previous layoffs, most of the people let go were poor performers. Now the company was letting go of great people who, through no fault of their own, got caught in a shift in strategy. The layoffs were very much on his mind when he dialed Joe's cell-phone number.

"You ready to get back into it?" Mike asked, when Joe answered the phone.

"Hooah, Bro," was Joe's now-predictable reply. They talked for a minute about where Joe was likely to be stationed, about the guys in his squad, and about how hard a time Joe's wife, Jennie, was having.

"So enough about me, Bro," Joe said. "I want to hear how your bounce is going."

"Overall, it's going great," said Mike. "I mean, really great. But I'm having to lay off thirty people out of five hundred. That's not so many, but they are really great people."

"I hear you, Bro," said Joe after a moment, "but just remember, you weren't given the option of taking really good care of five hundred people. You can either take really good care of four hundred seventy or take mediocre care of five hundred, and that's the only choice you've been given."

Joe always knows the right thing to say, Mike thought. Out loud, he said, "I just hope it doesn't hurt morale."

"Military morale or moron morale?" asked Joe. They

both laughed. "Look," Joe continued, "it's probably not so much a matter of *whether* you do layoffs as it is *how* you do them."

Mike took those words to heart. Over the next two weeks, he met face-to-face with every single person laid off. It was not an easy process, sitting with these valued employees as they went through a range of emotions: sadness, despair, anger, fear. When he could and they would let him, he tried to absorb their anxiety a bit. With each one, he offered to make phone calls to friends in the community, and even to customers and competitors, to explain the nature of the layoff and to recommend them for employment. The experience drained him emotionally, but it changed him in some very important ways. More than anything, it focused him like a laser beam on the company's performance. *Maybe if we can continue to keep disintegrating and reintegrating quickly enough, we'll never again have to say good-bye to so many people we like and respect.*

gift from kabul

the weeks and months flew by in a blur as Mike and his team began to build a company around their mission (the military kind). The product-development team quickly got a prototype up for the design Leslie's client wanted, and just weeks later, the customer placed a $10 million two-year order. On the strength of that contract, the sales team began demonstrating the design to other customers and prospects, and the company soon found itself trying to accelerate production to cope with a growing backlog. Sally and the operations group delivered on their commitment to roll out Lean Manufacturing companywide, exceeding cost reduction targets from the very first month.

Mike was so impressed by how effectively his larger group of executives, middle managers, and frontline people had solved the mission and money problems that he formalized an ongoing process that brought together forty people on a quarterly basis to disintegrate and reintegrate the company's approach. He even gave it a name: The RED (Reintegrate Every Day) process. He eventually brought

in a facilitator for the meetings to make sure that people
continued to take a full swing at the issues.

Mike was determined to spend less time getting the *right*
people and more time getting the *people right.* He elevated
the human resources function to the VP level and persuaded
Bill to take the position. It was a perfect fit. Through a
friend, Bill learned about a psychological profile the U.S.
military uses to select and train its commando units. The
test is designed to help people increase performance under
pressure, or to "manage their bounce." He persuaded Mike
to take the profile, and Mike was so impressed that he made
it available to the company's top fifty managers. Insights
from the tool quickly became a part of the language of the
company.

After a couple of months, Sean Tinsley noticed that while
the company was making great strides strategically, it was
falling down a bit on execution. He and his IT group quickly
created an Internet dashboard system to help people focus on
the 20 percent of activities that produce 80 percent of the
results. The numbers improved immediately.

Every week or two, Mike would get an e-mail from
Joe somewhere in Afghanistan, telling him of his latest
exploits. Occasionally Joe would attach a photo taken with
his cell phone, always of something ridiculous: Joe kissing a
goat by the side of some dirt road, Joe dancing on the mess
hall table in his boxers, or Joe holding two unidentifiable

Middle Eastern vegetables in front of him like two misshapen breasts.

Sometimes Joe's e-mails would be serious, like the one Mike received on March 22:

> **From:** GIJOE22123@yahoo.com
> **Sent:** Sunday, March 22, 2009, 1:44 AM
> **To:** Mike Maloney
> **Cc:**
>
> Mike,
>
> Just walked into the hut, haven't slept for 32 hrs. We got pinned down outside this little hamlet out side of Kabul, really in the shi**. Two of my guys got hit, our unit went to instant disintegration. Able to flank them and take them out, but it was one hairy bounce, man.

Mike closed his eyes and tried to picture his buddy, wedged into some dusty ravine, artillery fire kicking up showers of broken rock and smoke, men screaming and scrambling around.

The snow was completely gone in Boston on the bright spring day that Mike arrived back at the office after five to find a small square box wrapped in brown paper sitting on his desk with an Afghanistan return address. He tore open the paper and cut the tape on the top of the box, reached in, and brought out a racquetball that someone had

meticulously painted in desert camouflage colors. He fished
a card out of the box.

> Dude, *way* too much time on my hands over here.
> If the business world had Rangers, you'd be one of
> them. Keep bouncing, Bro.

Mike drove to the gym, dressed in the locker room, and
headed out the front door and across the parking lot in a
powerful stride. The air was crisp and strikingly clear as
he turned down Storrow Drive and headed up along the
Charles River, the same route he and Joe had taken that
snowy December night. He remembered the sight of Joe
gliding along, hood pulled up over his head, silly intersec-
tions of medical tape covering his purple nose. He pushed
his body hard as he crossed the river on Massachusetts
Avenue. He felt as though he could run forever. But it was
Gracie's birthday (her present, an Ebel watch, of course), and
Mary and the girls would be waiting for him to take them
out for a celebration dinner. His clothes were drenched as he
ran back across the parking lot, arriving at the same time as
another gym patron was approaching the door. Mike reached
for the handle and said, without thinking, "After you, Bro."
As the other guy stepped in, Mike stopped and watched his
reflection in the glass door slide back into view, his face
spread wide with a grin.

bouncing

the six key principles

bouncing: the six key principles

d rop a Christmas ornament and it shatters. Drop an orange and it bruises. Drop a hard-rubber ball and it bounces right back. As Sean pointed out in the story, these objects react differently to a sudden loss of altitude because they have different physical structures. In a similar way, organizations and people have varying levels of bounce. When faced with a competitive threat or economic downturn, some companies are like Christmas ornaments—they simply fall apart. When faced with a new challenge, some people will keep doing the same things they have done in the past, only harder and faster—surviving, but emerging from the experience as bruised as an orange dropped from a shopping cart. And some companies and people seem to have a rubber-ball capacity for bouncing right back. With each new challenge, they seem to grow only stronger and more resilient.

I'm not sure that someone can learn about bounce by simply reading a book. For me, the most powerful lessons on bounce came from my own times of disintegration and reintegration, like when I was at the helm of a company that had its own sudden drop in altitude that nearly killed it. The principles in this book are drawn largely from experiences like that and from my consulting with several hundred companies.

The story of Mike Maloney and his team highlights the six key principles that determine the quality of a person's personal bounce or an organization's bounce—whether it is a business, a nonprofit, or a government agency.

These principles can be thought of as concentric layers of a ball—each outer layer being dependent upon the layers underneath and creating increased levels of bounce.

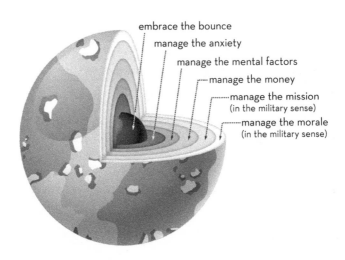

embrace the bounce
manage the anxiety
manage the mental factors
manage the money
manage the mission
(in the military sense)
manage the morale
(in the military sense)

For example, increasing bounce first requires that people or organizations "embrace the bounce," that is, accept this notion that environments are always changing in ways that require people and groups to adapt. Embracing the bounce leads to an understanding that anxiety can either help or hinder bounce—depending upon how you manage it. Effective management of anxiety sets you up to effectively manage money, mission, and morale.

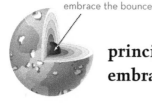

embrace the bounce

principle #1:
embrace the bounce

Life is adaptation, that is, repeated disintegration and reintegration in the face of change. It is not a question of *whether* you or your company will need to change; it is a matter of *when*—and whether, when faced with that sudden loss of altitude, you or your firm will be more like a Christmas ornament, an orange, or a rubber ball. Leaders especially need to embrace the bounce and need to focus on building "bounciness" into their organizations.

Reintegration

Disintegration

Another word for bounciness is *resilience.* When most
people think about resilient people or organizations, they
think of strength and hardiness, or of being particularly re-
sistant to stresses. In fact, evidence suggests that it is not
resistance to stress that makes people and organizations
resilient, but rather *adaptability in the face of stress.* I call
this the resilience paradox—over the long term, the most
resilient people and organizations are not necessarily those
characterized by a thick skin or an iron will; rather they are
those most able to disintegrate and reintegrate quickly and
successfully.

It often takes a jolt—what in the story I call a sudden loss of altitude—to get people's attention and prepare
them for some necessary change. That's because once you
become successful at something, a significant amount of
inertia builds up. You reach a steady state of success, and
lots of energy goes into reinforcing that steady state. After
all, the factors associated with the steady state are usually
responsible for your prior success! The problem is, as the
world changes, people or companies that don't change right
along with the world get left in the dust.

People who have spent their lives studying the psychology of resilience find that the most resilient people are good at giving up old ways of thinking (disintegration) and of adapting new ideas and approaches (reintegration).*

Although leaders cannot prevent their organizations from experiencing sudden losses in altitude, they have a significant amount of influence on both the *depth* and *duration* of the drop.

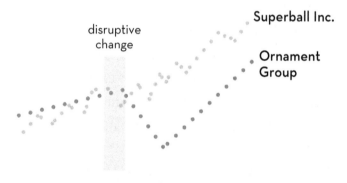

Consider the fate of the two companies above, the Ornament Group and Superball Inc., which serve customers in the same market.

---

*The model used here for "bouncing" is adapted from the classic book *Resilience: Discovering a New Strength at Times of Stress* (Hatherleigh Press), by Frederic Flach, one of the pioneers in thinking about what makes people resilient. He reasons that people, like organizations, have strong homeostatic impulses—a drive to "keep things the same." When they encounter severe or discontinuous change, they inevitably go through a period of disintegration followed by reintegration. Flach finds that resisting this process—due to either denial or nostalgia—may leave people or

The Ornament Group adopts an "if it ain't broke, don't fix it" point of view. Its leaders see the business as fairly simple and straightforward, and they operate with the belief that changes in customer needs and changes in the marketplace are usually exaggerated. As a result, when disruptive change happens, the Ornament Group, because of nostalgia and denial, has much farther to fall.

The leaders of Superball Inc., on the other hand, operate from the belief that factors outside a business (customer tastes, competitors, technologies) are always changing, and that companies need to adapt right along with them. In the words of former GE CEO Jack Welch, "When the change on the outside exceeds change on the inside, the end is in sight." So at Superball, employees are encouraged to spot trends that need to be addressed and even to question the fundamental assumptions upon which the firm is based. As a result, they are constantly finding some aspect of the firm to "disintegrate"—to rethink and revise—so that when disruptive change occurs, the company is better positioned to adapt.

The same holds for individuals. Dennis Charney, who has spent the better part of his life studying American prisoners of war, had this to say: "The art of raising resilient kids, and then resilient adults, is challenge and master, challenge and

---

organizations vulnerable to future stress and may lead to anxiety, depression, or stagnation.

master. You don't want to raise your kids stress-free because then they're not prepared—they're not equipped."

manage the anxiety

principle #2:
manage the anxiety

(absorb anxiety and turn anxiety 1 into anxiety 2)

The relationship between anxiety and personal or organizational performance is an interesting one. On one hand, anxiety can focus attention and motivate change. On the other hand, if there is too much of it, it can really hurt productivity and effectiveness. Leaders need to learn how to (1) absorb and contain anxiety when anxiety levels get too high and (2) master the art of turning one kind of anxiety into another.

Few people understand the importance of managing their own anxiety during times of stress. And few managers are adequately conscious of the role of leaders in absorbing anxiety when an organization meets difficult times. But the evidence is unmistakable: People who fail to manage anxiety are likely to find their capacity for productive adaptation markedly reduced.*

---

*For a fascinating overview of one recent scientific study on brain function under stress, see "In Hard Times, Fear Can Impair Decision Making," *New York Times*, December 6, 2008.

One of the most important things leaders should focus on in times of organizational stress is converting Anxiety 1 (people's fear of what might happen to them as a result of discontinuous change) to Anxiety 2 (people's fear of what might happen to them if they do not adapt to that change).* The subtle difference between the two is a hidden assumption: Persons or groups experiencing Anxiety 2 assume that they will have an important say in the eventual outcome. Leaders convert Anxiety 1 to Anxiety 2 by shifting the fear from "what might happen to us" to "what might happen to us if we don't change the path we are on." This is essentially what Mike did in the story when he suggested the "A, B, or C life" approach to his daughter's grades. Gracie's anxiety related to what her parents were likely to do to her. By setting up a system in which Gracie herself bore the consequences of her actions, he converted her Anxiety 1 to Anxiety 2, and she began to think and behave differently. The same thing can happen in organizations. People below the executive level often carry around incomplete or inaccurate mental models of the firm, which distort not only their thinking but also their actions.

---

*It was Ed Schein who introduced me to the idea that there may be more than one type of anxiety—specifically Anxiety 1 and Anxiety 2. In an article for the *MIT Sloan Management Review* ("How Can Organizations Learn Faster? The Challenge of Entering the Green Room"), Schein suggests that people and organizations adapt effectively during difficult times when the fear associated with *not* adapting (Anxiety 2) is greater than the fear associated with the risks of change (Anxiety 1).

Mike, by involving people at all levels of the organization
in a series of honest discussions about the condition of the
firm, shifted Anxiety 1 to Anxiety 2 and changed both the
thinking and the actions of his team members.

manage the mental factors

principle #3:
manage the mental factors

Skilled leaders know how to manage their own mental
processes in times of stress and how to help their teammates
do the same.

The tension in the huddle was palpable in the final
minutes of the 1989 Super Bowl game between the San
Francisco 49ers and the Cincinnati Bengals. The 49ers were
trailing 16–13 and pinned deep in their own territory,
on the eight-yard line. Returning to the huddle, 49er
quarterback Joe Montana drew a deep breath and poked his
head out of the huddle to look into the stands. Turning to
tackle Harris Barton, he shouted over the roar of the crowd,
"Hey, look, isn't that John Candy?" The team erupted in
headshaking laughter. Recalling that moment, many 49er
players who were on the field say that this was the precise
moment when they knew they would win. Montana then

led the team on a ninety-two-yard drive, throwing the winning touchdown with thirty-four seconds left. Montana demonstrated in that moment something he is still best known for today: As much as any player in recent history, he was able, even at times of great pressure, to keep things in perspective and to say the right thing at the right time to help his teammates do the same. In case you doubt this, remember that Montana had a total of thirty-one comeback wins in his career.

Managers wishing to lead their organizations through difficult times to triumph should follow Montana's example and become students of a key leadership question: During times of pressure, how does a leader help his team keep things in perspective and perform at its very best?

See things as they really are. People tend to do two things when facing pressure: They tend to revert to old ways of thinking and acting, and they tend to be influenced by a certain wishfulness, which may cause them to initially underestimate the seriousness of a situation. Mike fell into this trap in his marriage. His shame about his fear of failure caused him to stop sharing his life with his wife. He reminisced about happier times in Mexico rather than facing the fact that his marriage was in trouble. In the story, I refer to these twin threats as *nostalgia* and *denial.**

Nostalgia and denial were clearly present in the conference room as Maloney and his team struggled with the firm's problems. They yearned for the "good old days" when growth just seemed to happen—and they were eager to blame corporate or one another, while denying the fact that they had allowed their company to drift away from the market.

There are two things a person can do to make sure he doesn't fall prey to nostalgia or denial:

1. *Involve other people in thinking through the issues.* Until Mike talked to Mary, their relationship had no hope of getting back on track. Likewise, Mike and his group of senior executives remained stuck in their problem-solving efforts until they involved some other key people in the organization in their discussions. This is often the case in organizations: Senior executives "drink from the same data pipe" and often lack the rich, detailed knowledge they will need to help the firm adapt in the face of discontinuous change. In addition, some senior executives, wanting to leave the impression that their departments or divisions have it all together, may conceal the very weaknesses that need to be explored and addressed. Building a strategy team

---

*A classic study of the psychological roots of these tendencies can be found in Daniel Goleman's *Vital Lies, Simple Truths* (Simon & Schuster).

that brings together people from all levels can help a firm quickly get a handle on key issues and generate solutions.*

2. *Involve outsiders.* Many couples need more than a late-night talk around the kitchen table to build deep and lasting marital partnerships. Some seek the help of therapists and counselors, just as companies seek out consultants and advisors. The sociologist Georg Simmel has written extensively about the important role an outsider can play in helping people or groups identify areas where they have fallen prey to nostalgia or denial. Simmel says the outsider is "freer, practically and theoretically; he surveys conditions with less prejudice; his criteria for them are more general and more objective ideals; he is not tied down in his action by habit, piety, and precedent." In my previous book, *The Breakthrough Company,* I talk at length about the role of outsiders in two important chapters, "Erecting Scaffolding" and "Enlisting Insultants."

Treat causes, not symptoms. As Sally said in the story, sometimes the best advice can be "Don't just do something; stand there." Generally a crisis creates a sense of urgency

---

*For more on this subject, see my "Should You Build Strategy Like You Build Software?" *MIT Sloan Management Review,* Spring 2008.

that can help a leader mobilize people and resources to an extent he might not be able to during calmer times. But with this sense of urgency comes a trap: the tendency to rush decisions and to treat symptoms rather than causes. This is a particular temptation when it comes to matters of money, because difficult situations in personal or organizational life are often accompanied by financial problems. Sometimes decisions are made in haste to cut expenses, without adequate attention being given to *which* expenses, and *how* to cut them. Difficult times represent an opportunity for learning, growth, and development, but only if people are able to truly disintegrate and reintegrate, that is, go beyond just treating symptoms to identifying causes and addressing them.* Involving more people (as Mike Maloney did in the story) and getting outside assistance can help.

Emphasize a "we control" versus a "they control" mentality. You'll only be able to convert Anxiety 1 to Anxiety 2 to the extent that you are able to get people to recognize the control you really have over situations. People generally fall into two categories: those who tend to attribute outcomes to their own attitudes and actions

---

*See also my "Dig Before You Decide," Businessweek.com, March 15, 2006.

(I Controllers) and those who attribute outcomes to forces outside their control *(They Controllers)*. This result has been proved in research findings in a wide variety of settings, from studies of former POWs to Olympic athletes to children in immigrant communities.

Consider the difference between two sales managers explaining why their teams missed a quarterly sales forecast. The I Controller explains the failure this way: "Our team spent too much time chasing low-promise accounts. We need to do a better job of prioritizing next quarter." The They Controller, on the other hand, might explain the shortfall differently: "Top management has never given me the tools to be successful here." Note that the first sales manager attributes her failure to a *very specific cause within her control*—inadequate focus on the most promising accounts. The second sales manager, in contrast, assumes a They Controller posture and attributes the shortfall to a global cause outside his control—a general and vague lack of support by management.

A key job of leadership during difficult times is to encourage and reinforce I Controller thinking at the very time when people's fear and anxiety make them likely to look for someone else to blame. This was a key turning point for Mike Maloney and his team, the moment they realized that *they* were the people who had to take responsibility for where the business was, and the fact that, in the words of Einstein, "The significant problems we are facing cannot be solved at the same level of thinking we were at when we created them."

Hold hands in traffic. People naturally want to blame someone other than themselves in times of crisis. This tendency prompted me to include this fourth rule in managing the mental factors of resilience. I first heard the phrase "Hold hands in traffic" as I was getting to know the people at o2 ideas, an advertising agency in Birmingham, Alabama. Creative Director John Zimmerman showed me the firm's statement of company values, which contained two very interesting phrases: "Run to the sound of gunfire" (which I also included in the story of Mike Maloney) and "Hold hands in traffic." John explained to me that people in an advertising agency need to be ready to change directions at a moment's notice and that the "winner take all" nature of winning and losing clients tends to create a lot of uncertainty. To John, the motto "Hold hands in traffic" serves to remind people that it is in difficult times that they most need one another and most need to stick together. Leaders who are managing their way through a rough patch need to make sure their troops are shooting at the enemy and not at their fellow soldiers.

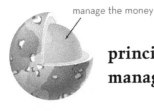

manage the money

principle #4:
manage the money

Several readers of the book's early drafts were surprised that
I had included a discussion of money into the story. But to
me, any discussion of bounce without a discussion of money
would be incomplete. That's because a company can have
a great mission, terrific morale, and enlightened leadership
capable of effectively managing the mental factors of
resilience but can still hit a rough patch and run out of
money. In both good times and bad, money—and specifically, an organization's ability to generate it by providing
clients with value—should always be a central concern,
whether it is a charity soliciting donations, a government
utilizing tax revenues, or a business selling a product.

When it comes to surviving and thriving in difficult
times, money can play three roles in the disintegration-
reintegration process: Money can serve as a *signal*, a *shock
absorber*, and also as a *strategic compass heading.*

Money is an important signal in difficult times because it
is often not until changes in the external environment have
actually impaired a firm's money-generating capabilities
that the firm is willing to acknowledge the need for internal

change. It was his company's declining financial performance that caused Mike Maloney and his team to look at their company and its clients from a new perspective. Mike was hesitant to talk about the growing financial problems with those outside the senior executive circle. This is a common mistake leaders make. But when he finally did raise the issue with the expanded group of middle managers and salespeople, their response was essentially "What took you so long?" The people in Mike's company had been seeing the signals for some time. Their anxiety grew as they watched key metrics decline and they saw that management was not taking decisive action. It is up to leaders to teach members of the organization that their ability to generate money by providing things that customers need is an important vital sign—in the same way that heart rate and blood pressure are important indicators of personal health. The better people understand this and the better they understand the impact their actions can have on the money-generating capability, the better positioned the company will be for bounce.

Money can provide an equally important signal to us in our personal lives. People who live beyond their means often discover that they are trying to make up for some perceived deficiency, or that they are spending in an attempt to distract themselves from some issue they need to address.

Money can also serve as a shock absorber. One of management's key tasks is to balance the drive to expand with the recognition that a certain amount of financial "slack" is necessary to protect the organization during a downturn. Companies operating close to the edge financially may lack the resources to absorb an external shock—and as a result may see their market position degrade during a downturn.* On the other hand, leaders who more effectively balance the drive to expand with the need to protect the organization during difficult times often have resources set aside that enable them to capitalize on opportunities during a downturn—such as hiring highly qualified employees who suddenly become available, getting deals on plant and capital equipment, and picking up customers from struggling competitors. It should also be remembered that using money as a shock absorber doesn't just mean taking a conservative tack in accumulating debt. Remember that Mike Maloney's team was able to accelerate the pace of adoption of Lean Manufacturing's production methods in a way that significantly cushioned the shock of what was happening in the marketplace.

Finally, money can provide a strategic compass heading

---

*See also my "Taking Advantage of a Down Market," Businessweek.com, April 21, 2008.

for the process of disintegration and reintegration. During good times, new projects and initiatives proliferate like barnacles on the hull of a ship, with little attention paid to whether they contribute to the firm's strategy or slow it down. As long as the wind is at the company's back, all is well. A dip in financial performance caused by a downturn presents the company with an opportunity to ruthlessly prioritize—to focus on the 20 percent of activities likely to generate 80 percent of the results. Maloney's team took a hard look at the customers and markets likely to generate the most value, and built the firm's strategy around them.

While Maloney and his team reduced costs *strategically,* many firms do not. Rather than doing the hard work of critically analyzing their company's business model (see **Treat causes, not symptoms,** page 147), many management teams take the easy way out and simply declare across-the-board expense cuts. Unfortunately this often results in a reduction of resources in the very areas of the firm that hold the best prospects for turning the business around. Another mistake managers commonly make is to underestimate the depth or duration of the downturn (see **See things as they really are,** page 145), requiring them to make serial expense cuts at great cost to organizational morale.

manage the mission

principle #5:
manage the mission
(in the military sense)

Do you have a mission in life? A sense of purpose that is the central organizing principle of everything you do? Research suggests that people with a strong sense of mission live longer, healthier, and happier lives. The same is true for organizations.

As Mike Maloney's team analyzed the company's financial problems (money), they discovered a *strategic compass heading* for redefining the firm's mission. And Mike learned in his conversations with Joe that *mission* is a military word—and that as the business world adopted the term, something important was lost in the translation.

As Joe said in the story, for a soldier, the mission is "everything." There is a sense of imperative inherent in the use of the term in a military setting, and an understanding among all that failure to achieve the mission may threaten the well-being of fellow soldiers or of the potential success of the greater cause for which the war is being fought.

Lots of companies have gone through some type of process to write a mission statement, but most do not truly have a mission—a highly specific, clearly stated, and widely embraced goal that carries with it a strong sense of the imperative. It is during a downturn that leaders have the rare opportunity to help an organization find its mission— that one thing that *must* be accomplished, regardless of the obstacles standing in the way. Mission is the thing upon which all the other things are based.

The path Mike Maloney's team took in redefining its mission is very similar to the path taken by the company at which I first served as CEO. It had enjoyed twelve years of uninterrupted success, developing into a fairly compli- cated business serving some 3,500 clients in ten industry segments from fifteen regional offices across the country. But shortly before I took over, a confluence of challenges in the market and in our internal operations threw us into a tailspin. Luckily, there were a number of key people in the firm willing to take an honest look at the situation. Like Maloney's team, we began with an in-depth look at the company's waning financial performance. And as in the story, we found out that the business was not making money where we thought it was. Further, we discovered that the industry niche in which we had the fewest number of clients actually represented our biggest opportunity for growth. These insights came not just from our senior executives, but also from a group of impressive middle managers who, when asked to assist in solving the firm's problems, exceeded even our wildest expectations. We ended up abandoning nine

of our ten industry segments to focus our attention solely
on the one in which we had the least amount of market
penetration—but where we felt we were positioned to be
able to produce exceptional value for customers. As a result,
our firm was able to increase revenues more than 1,000
percent in just three years.

It was not until we were able to articulate the mission
in very specific terms that we were able to really harness
the power of the idea. A good mission will almost always
identify what *market or markets* a company intends to serve
(for us, it was the telecommunications industry); which
customers within that market the company will go after (for
us, it was the large regional Bell operating companies and
major cable and satellite television companies); what *needs*
the company will try to fulfill (in our case, it was outsourced
customer contact and receivables management services);
and what the company's *unique value proposition* is (in our
situation, big telecommunications companies at the time
were throwing all their IT resources toward integrating
acquisitions and adapting to communication technology—
leaving them short on emerging technologies that would
enable them to more effectively interact with their customers
and optimize huge receivables portfolios). In other words,
know what hill you are going to take, and how you are going
to take it.

Perhaps the original military meaning of *mission* has

been lost in the modern mission statement because as firms grow larger and larger, leaders attempt to craft language that captures the full breadth of what a company is trying to do—and the language gets watered down in the process. Frankly, I'm not sure a mission statement, as it's currently defined, even makes sense at the corporate level of a huge conglomerate. Attempts to rationalize the "fit" of diversified business around a single statement are often tortured affairs. It's probably better to set mission at the business-unit level—where markets and customers and value provided can be more clearly delineated.

One final point: There has been significant discussion in recent years about whether firms should identify a mission for a long duration—with some suggesting that companies should look forward ten or even twenty years. This appears fanciful at best and is probably highly counterproductive. In today's rapidly changing environment, people tend to feel pretty disconnected from predictions made about the distant future. Leaders can't even predict what's likely to happen in the next three years, much less in twenty—and people in organizations know that. Better to stick to a time frame to which people can relate—say, two or three years—so that organization members are able to directly connect their actions in a given week or month to the mission the company is attempting to accomplish.

principle #6:
manage the morale
(in the military sense)

Like *mission,* the word *morale* also has military roots and
likewise has been hackneyed in its leap into usage in the
business world. In the military setting, the word means
"firmness in the face of danger, fatigue, and difficulties." So
when thinking about how to navigate difficult times, it is
useful to try to forget all the conventional wisdom regarding
what constitutes a "morale booster" and focus on one
question: What is it that gives people "firmness in the face
of difficulty?" The answer to that question points the way to
how we can most effectively build morale in ourselves and
in the people around us. Mike had seriously neglected his
own morale by shutting Mary out. On the other hand, he
knew himself well enough to realize what an important role
going to the gym played in helping to keep him balanced.

**People want strong, decisive leaders—but also leaders
who listen.** In the story, Paula's firmness was beginning
to waver as she walked into the office that night, worried
their division was going to miss a critical deadline to deliver
new cost cuts. In a matter of moments, Mike helped her

change her entire outlook. He'd called Rachel that morning and negotiated extra time to deliver their cost-cut plans, an action that Paula saw as strong and decisive—in fact, she was surprised he'd been able to get it done. He then told her he wasn't going to commit the division to a plan of action until he'd had a chance to work with his team on alternatives—in other words, until he'd had a chance to listen to his troops.

Leaders of organizations faced with difficult challenges need to understand that the urgency associated with those challenges often requires speedy decisions and actions. Nothing can damage morale more quickly than a leader who dithers, who seems unsure of himself or what to do. But at the same time, leaders who go off half-cocked or who change direction every couple of days will be equally unsettling to the troops. It's best to approach a challenging time as Mike Maloney did, striking a balance between decisive action and thoughtful consideration of the root issues—and remembering to address causes not symptoms.*

People want to be around others who see things as they are but who also keep one eye on the light at the end of the tunnel. Nothing causes morale to fall more

---

*See my "Front-Line Leadership," in which I outline management lessons from Henry V's battle at Agincourt, Businessweek.com, June 15, 2005.

quickly than a leader who is seen as suffering from nostalgia
or denial. Mike Maloney was on the verge of being seen in
this way when he called together his "last twenty people
on the boat." He learned that rank-and-file people in the
Sales, Operations, and IT departments had been debating
for months the company's declining performance on key
benchmark measures. They were worried that the people in
the executive suite might be asleep at the switch. Once it
was clear that the executive team was willing to face reality
head-on, the other people in the room voiced relief. *Now,
finally, we can do something about the situation,* they rea-
soned, shifting from Anxiety 1 to Anxiety 2.

But willingness to see things as they truly are shouldn't
be confused with giving in to hopelessness. It is one thing
to face a harsh reality, quite another to dwell on it. During
difficult times, people must encourage others to face the facts
squarely and at the same time strongly reinforce a belief in
their ability to solve whatever problems they are facing and
emerge even stronger as a result. The trick is to stress both
points at the same time. Dwell too much on the challenges,
and people may become discouraged and anxious. Shifting
too heavily into cheerleading mode can be equally dangerous;
too much rah-rah might suggest to people that you really
don't understand the depth of the problem. A measured,
honest, confident response to crisis is usually most effective.

People want to be surrounded by pragmatic people who are also people of character. During difficult times, difficult decisions will usually have to be made, such as temporary or permanent plant shutdowns, layoffs, product overhauls, and similar measures. Ironically, it's leaders who have the hardest time making tough decisions who often face the biggest challenges in effectively managing morale. That's because people aren't dumb: When tough decisions are overdue in an organization, people know it, and they know that the failure to make those tough decision might well put the company's future at risk.

In my own experience as a CEO, I once faced a situation in which, for my firm to survive, we needed to reduce our workforce by 75 percent. I am not a person for whom such tough decisions come naturally. Luckily, I had a great board member, who after a particularly difficult board meeting, put his hand on my shoulder and said, "Keith, you don't have the option of taking really good care of 100 percent of our people. You can take terrible care of 100 percent or really good care of 25 percent." I made the difficult decision, and the company survived.

But just as people in an organization want their leaders to be pragmatic, they also want leaders who demonstrate evenhandedness, and who, above all, show sincere empathy for people—both those who might be losing a job and those being called on to work extra hours to help turn the situation around. (For a more thorough treatment of character, see "Building Company Character" in my previous book, *The Breakthrough Company*.) As difficult as things became for him, Mike was a person of integrity, and that integrity attracted people to him and made them want to help him succeed—from Joe at the gym to his executive team to the people on the production line. He learned early in the story how to begin absorbing anxiety from his staff, and he showed that whatever challenges he faced, he was primarily interested in what was good for the company. Plus, he demonstrated real empathy, insisting on meeting with all departing staffers and spending time trying to help them find other employment. Mike was precisely the kind of leader people would be willing to follow into battle.*

One final point on managing morale: Any leader who takes complete responsibility for the morale of an organization is assuming more influence than is realistic and is setting himself up for failure. Morale is everyone's job. A leader can create the kind of environment in which unproductive anxiety is converted into productive anxiety, real issues are openly debated, and the root causes of problems are pursued and addressed. But it is the people in an organization who will, in the end, determine a company's morale.

---

*See also my "Four Mistakes Leaders Make When Downsizing," Businessweek.com, October 24, 2008.

acknowledgments

You can't learn everything you need to know about bounce by reading a book—you can only learn it by bouncing. Special thanks to Greg Suess, who first encouraged me to reflect on my own experiences bouncing.

The lessons here are largely a product of various bounces in my own life and career. I am particularly grateful to the people who accompanied me on the first and most important bounce of my business career, when I was a first-time CEO. As members of my board of directors, Tom Turney, Steve Carpenter, Jose Collazo, and Steve Olson all helped me to keep a steady hand on the tiller through some very troubled waters, as did advisors Don Clark, Don Rudkin, and Steve Hauck.

I also owe a debt of gratitude to "the last twenty people on the boat" at that company—including David Haynes, Steve Kent, Joel Lemos, Jim Montgomery, Gary Palatas, Chris Sutton, David Wright, and others. Their amazing commitment, compelling insights, and above all, abiding sense of humor at a time of incredible stress inspired much of the dialogue in the later sections of the book.

I am fortunate to have as my literary agent Esmond Harmsworth, one of the best minds in the business and what I am sure one would get if one crossed Merlin the

Magician with an English bulldog. Thanks also to my outstanding editor, Rick Horgan, and to the entire terrific team at Crown—publisher Tina Constable, publicity goddess Tara Gilbride, marketing guru Meredith McGinnis, and sales queen Jill Flaxman.

Two people deserve special recognition. John D. Nicks Jr. was an important mentor of mine during a particularly formative stage of my life. Joe Nicks in the story is named in honor of John, whose example remains the most powerful personification of courageous leadership I have ever observed or experienced. I also appreciate a lifetime of friendship with Alan Ludington, who over the years taught me many of the finer points of bouncing (and from whom I learned the A-B-C approach to parenting that Mike Maloney uses in the story).

A number of people provided comments on early drafts of this book and were quite helpful in refining these ideas. These include Matt Harris, David Haynes, Bob Hogan, Kent McClelland, Sarah Merz, Elaine Gause, Cary Chessick, U.S. Army Captain Johann Hindert, former USMC Staff Sergeant Mike Walker, and my two brothers, Kevin and Ken McFarland.

Finally, I appreciate my associates and partners at McFarland Strategy Partners, and our several hundred clients, who have over the past decade filled in many of the gaps in our thinking about what it takes to effectively bounce